The 30 Day Job Search Survival Guide

A Practical Step-by-Step Action Plan

Tré Rodriguez
Founder, Keep Working: Job Search Consulting, Global

The 30 Day Job Search Survival Guide

Contributors

The following individuals reviewed this content prior to publishing and their commentary was integrated to provide a well-rounded perspective.

April Starlight
Owner and Recruiter
Tangerine Search Inc.
San Francisco

Deborah Gavrin Frangquist
Career Counseling and Executive Coach
Chosen Futures
San Francisco

Sandy Cruze
Former Vice President, Technology, Alaska Tribal Health Consortium
Former Vice President, Quality, Risk Management Solutions
Former Director of Engineering, Google
Former Director of Quality, eBay
Former Director of QA/QC, Oracle
San Francisco

Nick Martinez
Strategic Marketing
Albuquerque

Anna Stein
Editor
Seattle

Luana C. Berger
Editor
Albuquerque

Tré Rodriguez

All Rights Reserved © 2020 Tré Rodriguez

First Printing 2020. No portion of this book may be reproduced, transmitted, reposted, duplicated, or otherwise used in any form or by any means, electronic or mechanical, without the express written approval of the author, except where permitted by law by reviewers who may quote brief excerpts in connection with a review.

ISBN: 9798669535056

Cover Design: Critical Eye
Interior Design: Critical Eye
Back Cover Photo: Critical Eye
Printed in the USA

Disclaimer and Terms of Use

All written content contained within is for information purposes only. Opinions expressed therein are solely those of Tré Rodriguez, Principal Consultant, Keep Working: Job Search Consulting. Material presented is believed to be from reliable resources and I make no representations as to its accuracy or completeness. Fee-only job search consulting services are offered through Keep Working: Job Search Consulting.

The 30 Day Job Search Survival Guide

Dedication

For Lily

Tré Rodriguez

Contents

Foreword	7
Introduction	8
A Note on Results	11
Day 1: Do Nothing	13
Day 2: Set Up a Routine	17
Day 3: Build Your Team	21
Day 4: Ideal Job Profile	25
Day 5: Informational Interview	29
Day 6: Get Resume Ready	36
Day 7: Get Active, Get Outdoors!	39
Day 8: Perfect Your Cover Letter Writing Skills	42
Day 9: Google Yourself	45
Day 10: LinkedIn Profile	48
Day 11: Personal Website	51
Day 12: Ask for Help	54
Day 13: Actual Job Searching	58
Day 14: Give Back	63
Day 15: Reach Out to Recruiters & Staffing Agencies	66
Day 16: Check-in with Yourself	70
Day 17: Get Social	76
Day 18: Continue Developing Yourself	79
Day 19: Read	84
Day 20: Polish Your Interview Skills	87
Day 21: Video Interview	94
Day 22: Confront Your Bias	99
Day 23: Turn the Tables	104
Day 24: Say Thank You!	109
Day 25: Prepare for the Salary Negotiation	113
Day 26: Prepare for the Counter Offer	117
Day 27: Professional Organizations & Certifications	122
Day 28: Relocation	126
Day 29: You Got Fired or Laid Off	130
Day 30: Final Review	134

The 30 Day Job Search Survival Guide

Afterward	147
Appendix A – Resources	149
Appendix B – Extra Tables	152

Tré Rodriguez

Foreword

Job searching can be daunting. In a decade as a recruiter, I've seen the challenges, the toll the hunt can take on candidates, as well as the overwhelming joy when a person gets the offer for a great job. I've known Tré for almost as long as I have been recruiting and have worked with many of her clients. She has had enormous success in coaching folks towards great opportunities. I've only ever encountered rave reviews about her job search services.

In this survival guide, Tré outlines many of the key points that will help set you up for success. How to be intentional when applying or reaching out for recommendations, practical things you can do in your daily search that will garner results.

The 30 Day Job Search Survival Guide

So many factors are out of your control when looking for a job, Tré has put together a great guide to help you do your best at the things that you can control. I hope this guide helps you and that you enjoy your journey!

April Starlight
Owner and Recruiter, Tangerine Search Inc.
San Francisco
www.tangerinesearch.net

Tré Rodriguez

Introduction

So, you find yourself in the job market. Maybe you got laid off. Maybe you decided to quit to escape an untenable situation. Maybe you had to relocate and are setting up roots in a new, or old, place. Maybe you just finished your bachelor's, master's, or Ph.D. Or a million other things that might have led you to this job searching place that you find yourself in. Either way, you've got your work cut out for you.

Did you know that job searching can be one of the most stressful times in a person's life? Does that mean that you're doomed? Absolutely not. It means that this is a time where extra attention and care around your situation is both warranted and worthwhile. The goal is to come out the other side better, or at least no worse, than before.

The good news is that there are specific strategies that you can take to make this process go more smoothly. This guide was created to give you pragmatic, actionable tips to make job searching easier to manage. Dare I say, enjoyable?

The 30 Day Job Search Survival Guide

You can read this guide in one day and then revisit one chapter per day for the next thirty days. You can skip around to the sections that you feel directly apply to you. You might choose to work through two or three chapters in one day and finish the whole guide within two weeks instead of a month. The important thing is to do what feels right to you.

Some of you will choose to read this guide more than once during the same job search or throughout many different job searches. I think this is an excellent idea and I encourage it. Learning, after all, is supported through repetition. I hope a lot of you will pass it along to your families, friends, and colleagues should they find themselves in the position to be job searching. My intention is to help as many people as possible with this material.

Remember that it is completely normal to feel a variety of emotions throughout your job search. Your feelings may change week by week, day by day, and sometimes hour by hour. This is not only completely fine, it is essential to becoming the newer, better professional that you are

Tré Rodriguez

meant to be. The important thing is not to resist these feelings. Just feel them and they will pass. Eventually, you might find them crystalizing into some new insights into yourself, your career, your industry, or your dreams.

If you find the material in this book useful, I would appreciate it if you could take a minute or two to leave a review on Amazon.com, Goodreads.com or whichever site you purchased the book from and use to track your reading. This helps more people find the book. Thank you!

The 30 Day Job Search Survival Guide

A Note on Results

Like most things in life, what you get out of this guide will be strongly linked to what you put into it. If you skim it, you might benefit from a few insights. If you read it front to back, you'll likely gain a bit more. If you do the work in every single chapter with focus and attention, you'll start to notice some nice changes. And if you decide to go the extra mile, read and rework the guide multiple times, you can expect many benefits to flow to you. The more times you read the guide, the more fully you will integrate the information and solidify the habits. It's all up to you and your level of commitment. I wrote the guide but I can't do the work for you.

The strategies in this book are meant to address some pretty heavy interior needs. I don't approach job searching as just a single dimensional problem but instead, focus on it holistically as a well-being issue. I know, from lots of experience, that this process can have some intense effects and so my goal is to make sure that I set you up for the best possible success.

Tré Rodriguez

Once you're finished, I would love to hear from you about additions you would like to see or about the amazing results you achieved as a result of implementing my suggestions. Please reach out to me! I will be very happy to hear from you.

www.linkedin.com/in/trerodriguez

The 30 Day Job Search Survival Guide

Day 1

Do Nothing

The first and most important step during a job search is to stay calm.

How could I suggest that you do nothing? Don't I know that you've just received a major shock? Your family is putting tons of pressure on you to, "get a job!" Every other article on the internet is admonishing you to, "follow your passion!" Your student loans need to be paid. Your bank account is getting dangerously low, or gulp is running into the negative. You've only got so much room left on your credit card. You need to move out of the place you're staying right now. It could be that your family is depending on you to pay the bills. Some of you will have a baby on the way or one in the crib. Maybe the food in the pantry is running scarily low.

Or maybe you're just going stir crazy from not having something productive to do for a while. You might be anxious to put your newly acquired skills to use while what you studied is still fresh. Perhaps you're ready to get out there on your own and make your mark on the world. It

Tré Rodriguez

could have been a while since you've had a steady paycheck and you're ready to start building those savings.

I get it. I've been there, in all kinds of situations. That's exactly why I am telling you to do nothing. Panicked or anxious actions are not usually our best actions. It's critical to stay level-headed. Which is easier said than done, right? But if this book has somehow found its way into your hands, I believe that you have a mind open to trying new strategies.

Today you're going to acknowledge all the pressures, excitement, and energies that are weighing upon you. You are going to accept them as part of the process. You are not going to rapid-fire shoot off one hundred emails with your resume attached to every job posting you can get your hands on. Nor are you going to beg anyone for their assistance. We need to be intentional about our job searching if we want to get the best results.

Again, if you've been job searching for a while or even if you've just been thinking about it for a while, I imagine that a lot of pressure has built up inside of you. If you have been laid off, fired, or otherwise suddenly displaced from

The 30 Day Job Search Survival Guide

employment you are most likely spinning with a ton of emotions, thoughts, and worries. Again, not our best state of mind to be job searching.

So today, think about the things you can do to relax. What activities put you in a good, positive frame of mind? Make a list of up to ten things that are proven to help you feel calm or happy. If you can't come up with them on your own it's OK to ask someone you know for suggestions or to do an internet search. However, do not include anything that doesn't genuinely work for you. This list is going to act like a lifeline as your search continues and you need to find ways to manage your mind-set through the process.

Tré Rodriguez

Day 1
10 Feel Good Activities

1.	6.
2.	7.
3.	8.
4.	9.
5.	10.

The 30 Day Job Search Survival Guide

Day 2

Set Up a Routine

"The secret of your success is found in your daily routine."
John C. Maxwell

One of the hardest parts of job searching can be how untethered it leaves you feeling. When you have a job or school to attend, your life cycles through a predictable set of events. You know what time to wake up, what time to eat, what time to leave the house, and what time to come home. Filling in the rest of the gaps happens somewhat automatically.

Job searching can be the exact opposite. Since you don't have to go to work, should you wake up at 7 am or 10 am? Should you go to bed at 9 pm or 1 am? When should you eat? What should you do first, second, or third?

This has, to say the very least, a disorienting effect on many job searchers. One thing you can do to stabilize yourself right away is to set up your routine. Just a set of daily activities that can make you feel grounded. I caution

Tré Rodriguez

you against setting up too detailed or too busy a schedule! That can be a sure way to fail. I'm not talking about a military-style regimen or a to-do list of one hundred items. I'm talking about four to eight daily activities that you can do at regular times each day to give you a foundation. An example of a daily routine might look like this:

1. Wake up with the sunlight ☐— not a big fan of alarms
2. Play with Kitty before exiting the bed — she insists
3. Make some coffee or tea
4. Wash the dishes from the day before
5. Make the bed
6. Turn on the computer to check-in with the internet
7. At some point during the day, depending on the weather, go for a thirty minute walk
8. Read a book for at least thirty minutes a day

Now nothing on that list is earth-shattering. These aren't world-conquering goals. What they do is they anchor us. Plus, the research about the benefits of making your bed every day is vast.

Your list might be completely different. It must be custom-tailored to you and your personality. Things that should be on your list are things that take care of your

The 30 Day Job Search Survival Guide

physical, mental, and emotional health. Also, it's important to build small wins into your routine — things that can make you feel good about yourself and give you a small sense of accomplishment. For me, that's bed-making and dish-washing. Make a draft routine here. Try it out for a few days and adjust as necessary. The important thing once you set it up is to practice it consistently.

Tré Rodriguez

Day 2
Daily Routine

1.	6.
2.	7.
3.	8.
4.	9.
5.	10.

The 30 Day Job Search Survival Guide

Day 3

Build Your Team

"If you want to go fast, go alone. If you want to go far, go together."
African Proverb

Another of the most challenging aspects of job searching is how isolating it can be. If you've just left a job or school, you are used to being surrounded by people. Even if you weren't talking to or collaborating with them all of the time, at least they were nearby.

It's really important to have someone to discuss the developments of your job search with. Usually, it's best if this person is not financially dependent on or supporting you. Also, exclude anyone to whom you owe money. People with financial ties will most likely have vested interests and may intentionally or unintentionally put additional pressure on you. This will not only stress you out but may influence your decisions contrary to your best interests.

So today your goal is to build your support network. Now if you already have one, great! Reach out to them

Tré Rodriguez

with a simple message to let them know that you've just started job searching again. Ask if it would be OK if you checked in with them periodically to let them know how it's going. That's it. At this time, you don't have to get into all of the details of how or why you found yourself in this position. The purpose here is to put your support network in place for future help.

If you don't have a support network, time to get thinking. Possible suggestions for whom you might include: a best friend, a former colleague, a mentor, an old professor with whom you got along well, a distant relative (like a cousin or an aunt), a former classmate, a clergy member, a team member, etc. Stay away from anyone who might be competitive with or jealous of you in any way. You don't need that kind of energy right now.

If for any reason you don't have someone you feel comfortable with or you just want more professional support, you can consider hiring a job search coach, a life coach, or a personal development coach. If your budget is tight you might be able to find free counseling at a local job or employment center. If you went to university you can check with your alma matter and see what services they

The 30 Day Job Search Survival Guide

offer. You might have a really good relationship with the staffing agency or recruiter that you end up working with and they could also be a fountain of support.

The intention here is to have several people, or at the very least one, that you can reach out to when you need someone to bounce ideas off. In the next table make a list of your support network. List their names and contact info.

Tré Rodriguez

Day 3
Support Network

Name	Number	Email
1.		
2.		
3.		
4.		
5.		

Day 4
Ideal Job Profile

"If you don't know what you are looking for how will you find it?"
Mike Biere

The number one barrier I see to my clients finding jobs that will make them happy is a lack of focus. Companies put together job postings because they know what kind of person they want to hire. You should do the same in reverse so that you know what companies to zero-in on and which to ignore.

You will then use this profile to evaluate everything else you do throughout your job search. Your resume, cover letter, LinkedIn profile, website, and interview should all be tailored around this ideal job profile.

Even though it seems like being very open-minded would broaden your opportunities to get hired, it paradoxically works against you. When you are not specific, you come across as unfocused or like you lack direction to hiring managers or people that you are asking for support from.

Tré Rodriguez

Think about it like dating. If you were asked out on a date by someone who said they were willing to date just about anyone… would that increase or decrease your interest in that person? If you asked them why they asked you on a date and they couldn't mention even a single reason, would you feel valued by that person and be encouraged to go on a second date with them? Maybe if you were desperate. In the long-term do you think that would work out well for you? Probably not. What if you asked your friends to set you up on a date and when they asked what kind of person you were looking for; you couldn't provide a single criterion? Some people might try to find someone but the likelihood that it would be a good match is low. A lot of people would listen and within a few hours or days forget about your request as they got caught up in their own busy lives.

Hiring managers and companies are not that different from a prospective date in this manner. Everyone wants to feel valued. They want to know that in a sea full of potential employers you chose them for definite reasons and characteristics that you valued. Not just because you didn't want to stay home on a Friday night, or better yet a

The 30 Day Job Search Survival Guide

Monday morning, but because you thought that together you could do great things.

It's important, critical even, that you do the work of figuring out what kind of place suits you best, a place where you can thrive. Is this easy? Nope. That's why it's so valuable and produces better results. Some of you might find this a difficult exercise to complete alone and if that's true for you, that's OK! Feel free to ask for the help of someone who knows you well, like a mentor. You might even consider hiring a career counselor or career coach.

Spend some time today and define the following criteria for your dream job. It's OK if this changes throughout your job search as you get a better idea of what you need. You should be updating this profile periodically as your understanding of what you want deepens. The important thing is to spend a decent amount of time reflecting. The better a job that you do in determining these factors, the easier it will be for you to find jobs that interest you. The key is that you are narrowing the pool of infinite options to those that will suit you best.

Tré Rodriguez

Day 4
Ideal Job Profile

Location:	Working on a team or working individually
Company size: big, medium, small	Working on-site, remotely, or a combination
Industry:	Liberal or conservative company culture
Type of service or product:	Identity group friendly, i.e LGBTQ, African American, immigrants, etc.
Job Title(s) :	Leadership profile that includes specific charactertistics, i.e. women, minorities, certain age groups, etc.
Reputation for something specific, i.e. giving back to the community, innovation, child-friendly, etc.	Other
Other	Other

The 30 Day Job Search Survival Guide

Day 5

Informational Interview

*If you want the best information,
go to the source.*

In an ideal world job searchers would have perfect information about what the jobs they are applying to are like and what the company culture is about. However, this is rarely the case. Several of my clients have interviewed for and accepted a job only to find out later that it was nothing like they expected! So, if this has happened to you, don't feel alone or put out.

If you have had this experience, you know how unpleasant or disheartening it can be. You likely want to avoid having it again. That's where informational interviews can save you a ton of time and energy!

The name states the purpose pretty clearly. Your objective is to interview someone to obtain as much information as you can about a particular job title, company, and/or industry. Think about the ideal job profile you created. Building on that, what questions might you

Tré Rodriguez

ask to find out if the job you are considering suits that criteria? Some questions might be direct. For example: how many women are managers in the XYZ department? Some won't be so obvious. For example, those dealing with company culture. Remember that sometimes stated company values don't always coincide perfectly with practiced values. Look up the Nike or Uber scandals.

This means that you'll have to put on your detective hat when crafting your questions and decoding the answers you receive. It will be as important to pay attention to what is said as well as to what isn't. In the following table make a few notes under your questions about what your ideal answers might include. For example, if you are asking the question, how does the department get along personality-wise? If you're extroverted and like being friends with your coworkers you might want to hear that they go out socially regularly after work. If you prefer to keep your work and personal life separated you might try to confirm that this is not the case. Because your ideal job profile is unique to you, there are no right or wrong answers per se. There are only answers that will encourage you to move toward or away from this company, industry, or job title.

The 30 Day Job Search Survival Guide

Here you want to make a list of ten questions you might ask a potential informational interviewee.

Tré Rodriguez

Day 5
Informational Interview Questions

1.

2.

3.

4.

5.

6.

The 30 Day Job Search Survival Guide

7.

8.

9.

10.

Tré Rodriguez

Next, think about the companies, industries, or roles that you are interested in working in. Who might you be able to interview to find out more about them? If you don't know anyone who is directly involved, how might you gain an introduction to someone there? If you can't think of a way, is it possible that a cold email or cold call might work? What do you have to lose? You might send a message like this to your contacts to solicit help gaining informational interviews:

> *Hi, Jose.*
>
> *I'm in the process of researching* **the oil industry/Shell Gas Company/Project Management** *roles and am hoping to conduct a few informational interviews to learn more. Do you happen to know anyone that you think I should talk to? I would greatly appreciate any introduction you might be able to make.*

Some options for finding people to do an informational interview with are: contacting the career placement or alumni association of your university, asking friends or family, or asking colleagues. I've had incredible luck

The 30 Day Job Search Survival Guide

connecting with alums from my universities through LinkedIn. If you decide on that route you might want to send a connection request with a message similar to this one:

> *Hi, Hitoshi.*
>
> *I noticed that you and I are both alumni from XYZ university. I was wondering if you wouldn't mind doing a short informational interview about **Chemical Engineering roles/the textile industry/consulting with Deloitte**? I promise not to take more than fifteen minutes of your time if you can do a phone call. I would appreciate it very much!"*

The most important things about conducting an informational interview are that you come prepared and that you do not overstep. Don't waste a person's time asking questions that you could have found the answers to via a routine Google search or read off the company's website. This will make you look lazy and unprofessional. Also, do not overstep by asking someone for help getting a job! Remember you requested an informational interview so your interviewee is not expecting to be hit up for a job.

Tré Rodriguez

Does this mean an informational interview won't lead to a job offer? No. If you make a positive impression on the person you speak with and form a genuine connection, the person might volunteer to help you with further steps. However, be mindful that this offer is initiated on their part with no pressure from you.

> **Recruiter Tip**: On LinkedIn you can use the search tool for companies of interest and filter it by second-degree connections. This way you know specifically who to ask. For example, you could write to your first-degree connection: "Hey Sarita, I saw that you're connected to Joaquin Martinez at Tesla through LinkedIn. I've been wanting to do an informational interview with someone there in Public Relations for a while. Is there any way you could make me an introduction? I'd greatly appreciate it! "

The 30 Day Job Search Survival Guide

Day 6
Get Resume Ready

Your resume is not for you, it's for them.

Some of you might keep your resume in tip-top shape at all times. Though many of you will not. It's OK if you don't. The key is to get started today.

Self-editing is notoriously difficult so it's extremely important that you get a second or third set of eyes on your document. No, you shouldn't do this all on your own. Even I still have a trusted group of people I send my documents to for feedback. No one is exempt. It's OK, important, and smart to ask for help.

You may choose to hire professional help or just get a few mentors or friends to weigh in. There is no right or wrong strategy here as long as the people you choose are dependable and have experience reviewing and writing resumes that get results. Don't be afraid to ask them about their experience before you implement their suggestions!

Tré Rodriguez

The fact is, the more defined your career, the easier it will be to write your resume. If you are a Marketing Specialist and you will be applying to all jobs Marketing… your job is pretty straightforward. The most challenging resumes to write are for those people who are changing careers or for people who have spent their lives acting as a jack or jane-of-all trades. Not impossible, but more challenging. For people in this situation, you may consider hiring or asking someone good at branding for help.

If your resume is more than one page, I strongly recommend you take a very close look at how much value those second, third, or fourth pages are offering. Remember that less is more, and brevity conveys mastery. Some of the most successful, experienced CEOs manage to get their resume onto one, or at the most, two pages.

The most important thing is to spend a good amount of time updating your resume to the latest standards which you'll need to research for your industry and geographic area. You can also ask about resume conventions during your informational interviews. Things change quickly so even one or two years can make a difference.

The 30 Day Job Search Survival Guide

Remember that your resume has multiple purposes. It gets you in the door for an interview, it provides talking points and structure during that interview, it justifies the person who decided to hire you to their bosses, and it smooths the way for your salary negotiation.

The final filter that you pass your resume through is: will my audience care about this? If the hiring manager, future boss, or future coworker will not find the item on your resume relevant to the decision they need to make… leave it off! Your resume is not for you, it's for them.

I'm not going to go into all of the details of the how and what to write in your resume. There are many guides on the internet or you can hire someone to help you. The point is, work on it today.

Tré Rodriguez

> **Recruiter Tip**: In the USA a resume and a CV are different. Resumes are a bulleted list of career highlights used to apply for most jobs and industries covering one to two pages. A Curriculum Vitae (CV) is a comprehensive document that spans many pages to detail a person's entire career and all professional accomplishments and training. They are typically used in academia and in cases where it is necessary to establish expertise.

The 30 Day Job Search Survival Guide

Day 7
Get Active, Get Outdoors!

"Look deep into nature and then you will understand everything better. "
Albert Einstein

> **Covid-19 Adaptation**: if you are using this guide during Covid-19 or another situation that does not allow you to physically gather socially, think of ways that you can adapt your interactions to follow the most recent safety requirements provided by your local authorities.

One of the things that people don't often talk about is how difficult it can be to keep a positive mindset during a job search. It's important to remember that when you make the shift from full-time employment or school, to job searching, many of you are not getting the same amount of positive feedback or interaction that you are used to. It can feel like you are uploading your resume into a black hole every time you apply to a new job. This will make a difference in your day-to-day state of mind.

Tré Rodriguez

When you're sending resume after resume and not getting many responses, or sometimes only negative responses, it takes its toll. Not just on you, but on most people! I have some tips to help you get a higher response rate on the applications you're putting in, and how to reach the right people, so don't worry. For right now, it's important to acknowledge that this is a normal part of job hunting and to take active measures to manage it.

One easy and accessible thing you can do to offset this lack of positive input is to go outside. Spend some time in the sun. Go take a barefoot walk in the grass. Look at some trees. Appreciate the flowers and other plants in your area.

If you love a certain sport, now is the time to engage in it. If you have an outdoor activity that you enjoy, like walking or gardening, this is a great time to practice it daily. Even if you just go sit outside and let the sunlight hit your face, arms, and legs, it will make a difference!

Today your goal is to identify at least five ways that you can be active and spend time outdoors doing something that you enjoy. If you want to do more feel free, but start

The 30 Day Job Search Survival Guide

with ten minutes as the bare minimum. Sitting outside on your phone or computer doesn't count! This is a time to unplug.

Tré Rodriguez

Day 7
Outdoor Activities

Covid-19 Adaptation: if you are using this guide during Covid-19 or another situation that does not allow you to physically gather socially, think of ways that you can adapt your interactions to follow the most recent safety requirements provided by your local authorities.

1.

2.

3.

4.

5.

The 30 Day Job Search Survival Guide

Day 8
Perfect Your Cover Letter Writing Skills

"A letter can make ordinary things important. "
Marilynne Robinson

Not all jobs request a cover letter, but for those that do, you can still get mileage out of writing a great one. Does this mean filling the page top to bottom with text repeating everything that is already in your resume? If you guessed no, you're on the right path.

In my experience with reviewing hundreds of cover letters, I can tell you that most of them would be greatly improved if the author reduced the text by at least twenty-five and often fifty percent. Today your goal is to research examples of great cover letters online and compare yours to decide if it's getting the job done.

Again, as with your resume, your guiding criteria must be: will this be a good read for the hiring manager or person to whom I send it? Worst case scenario, you write your cover letter for yourself. A better case scenario is that you write your cover letter keeping your audience in mind.

Tré Rodriguez

The best-case scenario is that you find a way to convey your passion and enthusiasm in a way that feels tailored to your audience.

Does this take extra time and attention? Absolutely. It also pays off.

Write three or four cover letter drafts and get feedback on them from people you trust and respect. Ask them which letter they find the most engaging, relevant, and well written. Integrate this feedback as you create your job applications.

> **Recruiter Note**: I don't work with cover letters, and when I receive one from an applicant, I just delete or ignore it. They're not used when applying to contract roles. Cover letters are still very important in the sciences, education, and non-profit industries.

The 30 Day Job Search Survival Guide

Day 8
Cover Letter Feedback Tracking

Cover Letter	Feedback From	Comments Made	X When Feedback Integrated
1.			
2.			
3.			
4.			

Tré Rodriguez

Day 9

Google Yourself

Look at your results and evaluate them through your potential audience's eyes.

You better believe that the hiring manager, recruiter, your potential coworkers, or your future boss are going to Google you. If you haven't checked out what results pop up when your name is searched, now is the time.

Ideally, the person who searches for you finds your professional, personal website, and your LinkedIn page within the first few results. What comes after that could be your other social media profiles such as Twitter, Facebook, Tumblr, Pinterest, etc. It doesn't matter too much as long as you don't have anything offensive showing up. If you have published works, awards, or other honors on industry-relevant sites, that's excellent!

How can you tell if something is offensive? Think of the most conservative person you know, maybe your mom or your grandma, finding those results and what their reaction might be. Do you feel uncomfortable?

The 30 Day Job Search Survival Guide

Now, this isn't to say that all people will have the same barometer of what is offensive. Your grandma might be a free spirit. Some of this will be industry-specific. If you're applying to be an investment banker on Wall Street versus a graphic designer for a skateboard company, obviously that's a different type of company culture and your potential coworkers will have different views as to what is acceptable.

The important thing here is to look at your results and evaluate them through your potential audience's eyes. If you're applying to a start-up company in San Francisco, what you see and how you interpret it will be different compared to a small insurance broker in the Midwest.

What do you do if you find something that you are worried would potentially turn off a future employer? If you have control over the material take it down or heighten your privacy settings. If you do not, contact the website and ask them to remove it. Depending on what the material is, this may be easy or very difficult to do. Start the process immediately.

Tré Rodriguez

> **Recruiter Tip:** If you have a serious issue with your search results, you can hire a public relations firm, or take steps on your own to get those search results moved to the second page on Google. Ninety-five percent of searches never go to page two!

The 30 Day Job Search Survival Guide

Day 10
LinkedIn Profile

"One out of every three professionals on the planet is on LinkedIn. "
Forbes

LinkedIn, as the Facebook of the professional world, is no longer an option. Everyone expects you to be on there. It is also no longer an option to have a bare-bones, I-signed-up-but-I-never-log-in, kind of profile. Least of all for job searchers!

The good news is that with some effort and self-study, you can create a great profile. Expect to spend at least eight hours working on it. There are tons of YouTube videos and online guides. You can also watch some of LinkedIn's tutorials.

If that's not your preferred method, you could ask someone you know for help or hire a career coach or counselor to guide you through the process. Whichever way you choose to approach it is fine, the important thing is to make a strong showing.

Tré Rodriguez

Take today to flesh out your profile. Go through each section of the profile edit options one by one and familiarize yourself with the latest updates. LinkedIn has gone through a lot of changes in the last couple of years so there are likely options that you haven't seen even if you've used it recently.

> **Recruiter Tip:** LinkedIn now has an area to indicate if you are actively looking for new opportunities that is only visible to recruiters on the back end. Make sure you have that box checked. Recruiters will be ten times more likely to reach out to you because they pay for every message that is not accepted. If they know you're open to new positions, you will likely be receptive to their InMail. You'll get contacted with new job opportunities that others will not, just from having that otherwise invisible indication on your profile.

Write an engaging summary in the first person that not only describes you as a professional but lets your personality shine through. Make sure to get some feedback on your summary from someone you respect and who has good writing skills. Fill out each job with pertinent details that would be both interesting and relevant to your audience. Make sure you have an eye-

The 30 Day Job Search Survival Guide

catching, professionally appropriate headshot and cover photo.

The goal is to make a stellar profile that you would be thrilled to have a hiring manager review.

Tré Rodriguez

> **Recruiter Tip:** Having a written recommendation from a prior manager makes your profile much stronger. Request one if you have someone who would be willing to write one for you.

Use this checklist to make sure you are covering the key elements of your LinkedIn profile. This list is not intended to be exhaustive.

Quick Start LinkedIn Profile Checklist

1.	Relevant or interesting cover photo	
2.	Excellent profile photo	
3.	Well written, first-person summary	
4.	Complete work history that addresses work gaps	
5.	Complete education section including honors	
6.	Organization memberships	
7.	Certificates	
8.	In-demand skills for endorsing	
9.	Customized profile link	
10.	Relevant profile heading	
11.	Interesting or relevant projects	
12.	Interesting or relevant coursework	
13.	Recommendations from colleagues, bosses, or clients	

The 30 Day Job Search Survival Guide

Day 11
Personal Website

"There's no shame in helping others see your value. "
Elissa Bertot

Personal websites are incredibly easy to make these days, and for that reason alone it's hard to justify not having one.

It's fine to make the first draft of your site a simple one that highlights your name, education, history, skill set, and what types of jobs interest you. You may or may not feel comfortable using a professionally appropriate photo of yourself. Do what feels right for you. Once you get further into the process, the temptation to tinker and expand your site will most likely overwhelm you. You'll find each iteration getting better and more interesting.

The benefit of a personal website is that you won't be limited in the same way that you are on standardized social media profiles. It is an opportunity to convey your personality and style.

Tré Rodriguez

You can choose to present yourself via text, audio, video, photos, or some combination. Some of you might hire someone to make your site although that is not necessary. When building your webpage, revisit your ideal job profile and think about what hiring managers and coworkers would enjoy seeing from you. Let this guide your choices for content.

Here's a website I like:

nicholasmtz.com

Nick's website is aesthetically pleasing, easy to navigate, provides all of the relevant information, and has a unique personal touch. He includes both web and PDF versions of his resume as well as a list of core competencies, a portfolio of his work, and testimonials. Additionally, he proactively addresses a work gap in his experience in a way that is compelling and hard not to understand. If a hiring manager or recruiter were to browse to this page, they'd be supported in their decision to bring Nick in for an interview or reaffirmed in their decision to make him an offer. That is exactly what you want your site to achieve.

The 30 Day Job Search Survival Guide

Take some time today to research at least three personal websites of people you know, people in your industry, or professionals in any realm. Make some notes about what you like about their sites to get ideas for building your own.

Tré Rodriguez

Day 11
Personal Websites I Like

	Address	What I Like
1.		
2.		
3.		

Use this checklist to get started. This is in not meant to be an exhaustive list.

Personal Website Checklist

1.	Website address:	
2.	Your name as listed on your resume, LinkedIn, etc.	
3.	Your photo – if using	
4.	Your education and training	
5.	Your preferred job title(s) and industry(ies)	
6.	Your resume in PDF	
7.	List of your top skills	
8.	Recommendations for your work	
9.	Examples of your work, if able	
10.	Links to your relevant social media	
11.	Links to relevant content owned by you	
12.	Links to relevant content not owned by you	

The 30 Day Job Search Survival Guide

Day 12

Ask for help

No one achieves anything great in this world alone.

> **Recruiter Tip:** Remember, humans are social animals who feel good when helping others. Most people are not only willing to lend a hand, but experience a very rewarding feeling from doing so. Don't think of your request as a burden, but an opportunity to share tangibly!

The myth of the self-made person is just that, a myth. Everyone gets help somewhere along the way.

It is especially critical to get comfortable asking for help during your job search because, as you may have read, the best positions are advertised after they've already been filled. To avoid spinning your wheels and wasting your energy, do everything you possibly can to get your resume in the hands of a human being and not lost in some online applicant tracking system.

Tré Rodriguez

If you have any qualms about wasting your connections' time, remember that many companies offer their employees bonuses for bringing in qualified candidates. Sometimes these bonuses can add up to a couple of thousand dollars. So really, asking for help can be a win-win situation. Especially if that person is convinced of your enthusiasm and dedication.

> **Recruiter Tip:** As mentioned earlier, a lot of applications entered online are simply never viewed by the recruiter, or HR person, who is screening resumes for a role. They are often overwhelmed by the volume of responses to a single position or find themselves sifting through resumes that are a total mismatch for their positions — truck drivers applying to software engineering roles and the like. Over sixty percent of open jobs are never posted publicly but instead filled via referral or from the recruiter searching on a resume posting site or LinkedIn.

Gather a list of all your contacts. They could be school connections, former colleagues, friends, mentors, etc. The broader your list the better. You'll send them a simple, direct email and attach your resume. Your goal is to make it as easy as possible for them to help you. Of course, tailor this message to suit your personality, style, and

The 30 Day Job Search Survival Guide

relationship to the recipient. The bolded words would be changed to fit your specific situation. Also, remember that shorter messages are better than longer ones.

Tré Rodriguez

Dear Darius,

Thank you for taking the time to open this message. I know you are busy so I really appreciate your attention. I am writing to let you know that I've recently re-entered the job market and I'd like to ask for your support.

I'm very enthusiastic about finding the next role that I can thrive in. Specifically, I am looking for **Marketing Specialist** or **Business Development** roles in the **Technology** sector. I have 10 years of experience in **SaaS** and particularly enjoy products that deal with **education** and the **environment**. My dream companies to work for are **Leapfrog, Udemy**, and **Coursera**. If I could find a role in one of those companies or a similar company, I might die of happiness.

If you are willing to share any contacts, ideas, or suggestions that might assist me in pursuing these kinds of roles or companies, I would be eternally grateful. Of course, I would look forward with anticipation of returning the favor. I've attached my resume to make it as easy as possible for you to help if you are able. I'd also like to ask for your permission to follow-up in a few weeks and let you know about my progress.

Thank you so much for your consideration.

The 30 Day Job Search Survival Guide

Day 12
Asking for Help Check List

1.	Gather contacts from:	
	K-12	
	college or university if attended	
	previous jobs	
	community connections	
	family	
	any other social contacts	
2.	Draft an email using the example above	
3.	Complete email using information from ideal job profile	
4.	Send email in batches grouped by relevance	
5.	Select day to follow-up with contacts	
6.	Follow-up	
7.	Record any leads and follow them	
8.	Say thank you to anyone who provided help	
9.	Say thank you to anyone who provided encouragement	

Tré Rodriguez

Day 13
Actual Job Searching

Job searching is quality over quantity.

Do not, I repeat, do not spend eight hours a day job searching. This is a surefire way to burn out and decrease the quality of your efforts. Also, don't even think about rapid-fire sending off ten or twenty resumes in one day.

I cannot tell you how often job searchers tell me that they are doing everything they can by applying to every job that comes across their path. Unfortunately, this produces a false sense of productivity. This might sound harsh but it needs to be said: this is a great way to waste your time. Our goal is to produce results, not to show busy work or effort.

Job searching is a quality over quantity game. If you play the numbers game and apply to everything you've ever heard of… you might get a job, but it's highly improbable that you will be happy or satisfied in that role for very long. Most likely you will just waste your time and the time of many companies.

The 30 Day Job Search Survival Guide

The fact is that it takes just as much energy and effort to go after a company or a role that you really want as it does to pursue a ton of jobs that you are barely interested in half-heartedly. It's a no-brainer which one produces better results in the long run.

Does that mean that you won't have to take a job that you aren't crazy about to make ends meet? Not necessarily. This is real life and if you have to put food on the table and pay the rent or mortgage, then that's what you need to do. However, the goal is not to get stuck in that kind of job for very long. One way to avoid this is to make sure you are pursuing a job that makes you happy. Will that job be perfect? No job ever is. Yet it is very possible to find one that you enjoy a majority of the time if you do it right.

Your goal should be to job search, or do job-search related activities, for no more than four hours a day. Do you know who else worked in four-hour blocks? Many of the most accomplished geniuses throughout history.

Tré Rodriguez

Limiting your job search efforts to four hours a day forces you to become more efficient and focused. As we know, the task expands to fill the space given. So, if you give yourself eight hours, you will find a way to work less efficiently for eight hours. This will take a toll on your mental and emotional health.

Instead, I strongly encourage you to go in there like a marine. Get in, get it done, and get out. Have a list of things you need to accomplish in those four hours and knock it out.

An example list might look something like this:

1. Research and apply to the Clorox company:
    a. Review website completely
    b. Search for latest news dealing with Clorox
    c. Search and study at least 10 Clorox employees on LinkedIn in the area of interest to see what their background is
    d. Search to see if I have any contacts at Clorox that can make an introduction
    e. Try to get an informational interview with someone who works or has worked at Clorox and ask them questions about culture, fit, and

The 30 Day Job Search Survival Guide

          working environment — do not ask them for help getting a job

  f. Find two of the best-fit job postings at Clorox

  g. Tailor resume to Clorox style

  h. Tailor cover letter to Clorox specific details

You might not accomplish all of those things in four hours. Great! Leave the ones you don't finish for the next day. I cannot stress this enough: every application you submit should be quality over quantity. Does this take significantly more time per application? Absolutely. That's why it produces better results.

This next part is important: some of you will feel a certain level of guilt if you aren't spending every waking moment job searching. Maybe you've got someone in your life putting a lot of pressure on you to, "just get a job already!" I understand how you feel.

The thing to remember is that these strategies are focused on producing results, not just making you look or feel accomplished, but actually leading you to accomplishment. If you trust and work the system, you'll eventually see it for yourself.

Tré Rodriguez

Your goal is to increase your return rate. If sending out ten to twenty resumes a day has you getting a ten percent return rate, aim to increase that to fifty percent by sending out one tailored resume every two days. Quality over quantity.

Complete the relevant checklist items on the following page. Add any additional steps in the blank rows.

The 30 Day Job Search Survival Guide

Day 13
Job Search Action Plan Check List

1.	Research and apply to the _____ company	
2.	Review _____ website completely	
3.	Search for latest news dealing with _____	
4.	Search and study at least 10 _____ employees on LinkedIn in the area of interest to see what their background is	
5.	Search to see if I have any contacts at _____ that can make me an introduction	
6.	Try to get an informational interview with someone who works or has worked at _____ and ask them questions about culture, fit, and working environment — do not ask them for help getting a job	
7.	Find two of the best-fit job postings at _____	
8.	Tailor resume to _____ style	
9.	Tailor cover letter to _____ specific details	
10.		
11.		
12.		
13.		
14.		

Tré Rodriguez

Day 14
Give Back

"If you are feeling down, unmotivated, or depressed, immediately stop what you are doing and go find someone worse off than you are to help."
Dali Lama

Sometimes when we are facing difficult challenges it can be hard to remember how well-off we are and to not focus on the things that are not going our way. This is pretty natural as evolution primed us to pay more attention to the negative than to the positive for survival. So, if you find yourself doing that during your job search don't beat yourself up about it. However, it is important to take steps to mitigate the impact.

One of the best ways to improve our spirits is to do something that benefits someone else. No matter how bad our situation is we can always find someone who is having a hard time in some way that we are not. Helping that person can make a difference in both our lives and theirs.

Maybe you don't have a job, but you can watch your sister's kid for a few hours this week so that she can have

The 30 Day Job Search Survival Guide

a much-needed break. You could give your neighbor a ride to the grocery store. You can volunteer at a soup kitchen in your town. You could coach your son's little league team this summer. You might help your cousin with their homework.

I want to clarify that the purpose is to give a small boost of help, not to assume responsibility for another individual's circumstances or use this as a way to procrastinate solving our own problems.

Make a list of at least ten people whom you could help in the next month. You don't have to do everything today; you can go at your own pace. The important thing is to contribute where and when you can!

Tré Rodriguez

Day 14
Paying It Forward List

Person, family, or group	What they need	How I can help
1.		
2.		
3.		
4.		
5.		
6.		
7.		
8.		
9.		
10.		

The 30 Day Job Search Survival Guide

Day 15
Reach Out to Recruiters and Staffing Agencies

A great recruiter can make all the difference in results and uncovering opportunities that you may not have thought about, heard of, or even considered!

A lot of success is tied directly to one principle: leverage. What you can do alone is no comparison to what you can get accomplished if you use the right tools and resources. This is where recruiters and staffing agencies can become invaluable.

Recruiting has a somewhat deserved reputation for being horrible. I'm not going to lie and say that over the years I haven't come into contact with some truly awful recruiters. However, I can also honestly and truly say that some of the recruiters I know are some of the best, brightest, and most helpful professionals I've met. The key is to get connected to the good ones.

A great recruiter can make all the difference in results and uncovering opportunities that you may not have thought about, heard of, or even considered! A good recruiter can be a rich resource of feedback, support, and

Tré Rodriguez

encouragement throughout your job search. They can offer great coaching and tips.

> **Recruiter Tip:** Consider reaching out to HR or recruitment people at the company where you are applying, even if you don't know them. Find out who is hiring for the role. See who the job poster is. You can also look on LinkedIn to see if you can deduce who the recruiter might be, then call them. Pick up the phone, dial the mainline, and ask to be connected to that person. When they answer tell them you've just applied and are a great candidate for three specific reasons. You have A, B, C experience desired for the role, and you are perfect for the job. You can also leave a voicemail, just make sure to clearly leave your call-back number. If you can't reach them by phone, shoot them an invite to connect on LinkedIn with a similar message.

Ask the people you know if they have worked with a recruiter they loved. When considering whether to work with someone check out their LinkedIn profile and see what kind of recommendations their former clients have given them. If you are working with a career counselor or coach, ask them if they can introduce you to someone they like. You can do the same thing with staffing agencies.

The 30 Day Job Search Survival Guide

Staffing agencies have the additional benefit of being industry specific in some cases. They can be a great way to get into a position quickly if you are under intense financial pressure. They can help you find a temp role to act as a stepping stone until you find something that is a better fit. With temp-to-hire positions, you can test out a role to see if you like it before committing.

> **Recruiter Tip:** When you apply to a position through a staffing firm, you will be one of a much smaller pool of applicants. Often this means being one of twenty resumes the manager will see, rather than just one resume out of several hundred that came in via a job posting. In addition, most recruiters earn a commission by placing people in jobs, so they will do everything they can to help you get the job. They will apply their depth of knowledge of their client to this aim. The recruiter may be familiar with internal workings at the company you're applying to or know the personality of the manager who will be interviewing you, and help position you in the best possible light to fill their need.

Make a list of recruiters and staffing agencies that you can contact. Gather names from internet research,

Tré Rodriguez

recommendations, LinkedIn, etc. Make a plan to check-in with them periodically about opportunities. Recruiters are busy so it pays to ping them every once in a while, just be prudent to not harass them, to stay top of mind!

The 30 Day Job Search Survival Guide

Day 15
Recruiter and Staffing Agency Contact List

Found via	Company	Contact	Email / Phone	Follow Up	Follow Up	Follow Up

Tré Rodriguez

Day 16

Check-In with Yourself

"Self-knowledge is the beginning of self-improvement."
Baltasar Gracian

During a job search, you have a lot of new and different experiences. It's important to take some time to reflect on all that is happening; all that you are learning and feeling through the process. This will make you a more self-aware person, a better employee, and more effective in your job search.

Today you are going to answer the following questions to review the steps of the last fifteen chapters and evaluate how things are going. The more completely and accurately you answer these questions, the better results you will get throughout this process.

The 30 Day Job Search Survival Guide

Day 16
Halfway Check-In Accountability Questionnaire

Ch.	Topic	Question	Your Comments & Adjustments
1.	*Do Nothing*	Are the activities that you chose supporting you in staying calm and happy? If not, what can you change to make them more effective?	
2.	*Set-Up a Routine*	Have you been keeping your routine? Does it help? If not, what adjustments can you make that will work better?	
3.	*Build Your Team*	Are the people on your list available and supportive? Have you called on them and received satisfactory responses? If not, do you need to adjust your list or change your approach?	

Tré Rodriguez

4.	*Ideal Job Profile*	It's time to update your ideal job profile with the new information you've learned or identified through this process. What has changed or become more specific for you?	
5.	*Informational Interview*	Have you been able to conduct at least one informational interview? If not, why not? What can you do to ensure that you are taking this valuable step? If you have conducted interview(s), what have you learned?	
6.	*Resume*	Have you updated your resume? Did you ask anyone for feedback and did you make improvements based on their commentary? If not, what can you do to move forward?	

The 30 Day Job Search Survival Guide

7.	*Get Active, Get Outdoors*	Have you been able to spend at least 10 minutes per day outdoors? If not, why not? Does your list of activities need to be updated with items that will motivate you more? Could adding a partner to your activities help? How can you ensure this will happen?	
8.	*Cover Letter*	Did you make at least three cover letter drafts and get feedback on them from people you trust? If not, why not? What can you do to be sure that you are getting the CL practice you need?	
9.	*Google Yourself*	Did you Google yourself? Were the results satisfactory? If not, what actions have you taken to improve them?	

Tré Rodriguez

10.	*LinkedIn Profile*	How does your LinkedIn profile look? Did you spend at least eight hours updating it and making sure that it is complete and as polished as possible? If not, why not?	
11.	*Personal Website*	Have you made a simple personal website to improve your search results and online presence? If not, what is holding you back? What can you do today to start the process?	
12.	*Ask for Help*	Have you sent an email to all of your contacts asking for support? If yes, what were the results? Have you followed up on any offered help? If no, what stopped you and how can you push past it?	

The 30 Day Job Search Survival Guide

13.	Actual Job Searching	How is your job searching going? How often are you applying to jobs? Are you reaching at least a 30% return rate on resumes submitted? If not, what can you do to improve your return rate?	
14.	Give Back	Have you identified ten people, groups, or organizations that need your help? Have you contributed in some way, however small, to at least one of them? If not, why not?	
15.	Recruiters & Staffing Agencies	Have you contacted at least one staffing agency or recruiter? If not, why not?	

Tré Rodriguez

Day 17

Get Social

A fringe benefit of social participation is that you might hear about jobs and opportunities through your connections that you might not have heard about otherwise!

> **Covid-19 Adaptation**: if you are using this guide during Covid-19 or another situation that does not allow you to physically gather socially, think of ways that you can adapt your interactions. Can you use the phone, video conferencing, chat groups, or other tools to achieve similar goals?

So, I already mentioned that you are only going to be job searching for four hours a day. What are you supposed to do with the rest of your time? If you answered sitting on the couch watching Netflix or spending hours on the web… wrong!

One thing that you have lost in making the transition from employee or student to job searcher is your opportunity for social interaction through those roles. Now if you are a member of a club or a sports team, hopefully, you have already realized the importance of those

The 30 Day Job Search Survival Guide

interactions! If not, now is the time to consider joining a team or club.

This is important for many reasons. The biggest is that it will help you manage your state of mind. Remember, if all goes right, you are going to be sitting in front of interviewers convincing them that you will be a good, enjoyable employee to have around. The better you feel about yourself, the easier that will be. So, spend time with people! Or if you're an introvert, near people is also OK. One of my favorite introvert activities is to go be kind-of-social by reading or painting in a cafe. The people are there, but I don't have the pressure to interact with them directly.

Something you might do is to join a local community sports team, an affinity club, a book club, a church, a synagogue, or a community group. There are tons of options and you can surely find one to suit your preferred level of engagement and interests. Whether you choose to participate once a week or more is completely up to your budget, availability, and preference, so tailor your plan to you.

Tré Rodriguez

Make a list of four social activities that you can participate in regularly during your job search:

The 30 Day Job Search Survival Guide

Day 17
Social Activities

Covid-19 Adaptation: if you are using this guide during Covid-19 or another situation that does not allow you to physically gather socially, think of ways that you can adapt your interactions. Can you use the phone, video conferencing, chat groups, or other tools to achieve similar goals?

Activity	Day + Time
1.	
2.	
3.	
4.	

Tré Rodriguez

Day 18

Continue Developing Yourself

"Read information in your field for at least one hour per day. This habit will eventually make you one of the most knowledgeable people in your business."
Brian Tracy

There are two principal reasons for continuing to develop yourself during the job search. One is for your mental health. Having something to learn and continuing to grow will give you some of those small wins I talked about on day two. It will give you something else to focus on instead of job hunting. Keeping your mind sharp is always a good idea.

The second is so that if your interviewer asks what you've been doing for the past few weeks or months, you can talk about how you are continuing to stay up to date in your field. You can mention the database analysis class or the digital marketing course that you are taking. You can talk about the book on algorithms that you're reading or the sales university extension course that you just completed. Hiring interviewers will like to hear that you are a person committed to personal growth.

The 30 Day Job Search Survival Guide

Today your job is to research the most wanted skills for job applicants in general, and the most wanted skills in your specific industry.

Tré Rodriguez

Day 18
Most Wanted General Skills

1.	3.	5.
2.	4.	6.

Most Wanted Industry Skills

1.	3.	5.
2.	4.	6.

Take an honest assessment of your own skillset and notice which ones from these lists that you are lacking or that need to be increased. If you aren't sure, you can ask someone who has worked with you. Next, choose one skill from each of those lists that you will dedicate yourself to mastering. Once you finish those two, you can begin

The 30 Day Job Search Survival Guide

another two. Continue working in sets of two for as long as your job search lasts or indefinitely if you prefer.

In the next table identify six different ways you can develop the selected skills. Some examples, with various associated costs for all budgets, are LinkedIn courses, Udemy, Coursera, your local community college, the library, hiring a private tutor, etc. Then choose one or two and get started! Plan to devote at least three hours a week to personal development.

Tré Rodriguez

Day 18
Skills I Want to Gain or Improve

1.	2.

How I Can Gain These Skills

1.	3.	5.
2.	4.	6.

The 30 Day Job Search Survival Guide

Day 19
Read

"A little reading is all the therapy a person needs sometimes."
Unknown

Those of you who know me know I am an avid reader. Most leaders are. Reading has so many benefits and there are so many different things to read that there are few reasons not to. Anyone can find something they would enjoy with a little effort.

Reasons for reading during your job search:

1. Reading increases your attention span and improves your focus -- a huge benefit in a world plagued by smartphones, distractions, and instant gratification.
2. Reading improves your memory.
3. Reading fosters your ability to make connections between different fields and ideas.
4. Reading is a proven avenue to furthering your expertise.
5. Reading decreases stress, helping you to relax.
6. Reading fiction improves your emotional intelligence – which is one of the most in-demand skills.

Tré Rodriguez

Your goal is to read at least ten pages a day of any printed material — this should take you about thirty to forty-five minutes depending on the difficulty of the text and your reading speed.

The guidelines are as follows: no reading on your phone or computer if at all possible. A Kindle or electronic book is fine. The best thing would be to turn your phone on silent while you are reading. If you have children or a situation that requires you to be available that is, of course, an exception. The point is, to be honest with yourself. You know you are not getting the best reading time if you stop every paragraph to check Twitter, Facebook, etc.

What you choose to read is totally up to you. You can read fiction or nonfiction, something related to your industry or not. You can read something from the Modern Library's most esteemed lists, a bestseller, or a romance novel. The choice is yours. Just turn those pages, at least ten of them, every day. Start today.

The 30 Day Job Search Survival Guide

Make a list of ten books or publications that you'd like to read below. You could find these books on your shelf, get recommendations from a friend, search a list on the internet, or visit the local library or the nearest book store. No one needs to approve of this list but you.

Tré Rodriguez

Day 19
Reading List

1.	6.
2.	7.
3.	8.
4.	9.
5.	10.

The 30 Day Job Search Survival Guide

Day 20
Polish Your Interview Skills

"A job interview is not a test of your knowledge, but your ability to use it at the right time."
Unknown

It's a fact that very few scenarios in life reflect the job interview, often least of all the actual job you will be doing. Industries are starting to recognize that the standard job interview is not the best tool for evaluating how well a candidate will perform.

However, until wide-sweeping changes occur, you will have to deal with them. So, it's in your best interest to perfect your skills.

The first step is to research what kinds of questions are most commonly asked for the type of role and industry you will be pursuing. Create a list of ten to fifteen questions you think will likely be asked. Enter in your desired job title and industry into Google and see what comes up. Next, add the name of one of your ideal companies. Dig around, following the links, and see what options you can find. As you go on interviews you can also add the particularly

Tré Rodriguez

interesting, challenging, or relevant questions you receive to this list.

You might be tempted to skip this step. Don't. The research combined with the act of writing your questions down will start your mind thinking about potential answers and relevant stories. Practice makes perfect.

> **Recruiter Tip:** You should be sure to include questions from the following purpose categories: verifying skills, abilities, understanding your values, brainteasers, teamwork, cultural fit, and problem-solving style.

The 30 Day Job Search Survival Guide

Day 20
Potential Interview Questions

1.

2.

3.

4.

5.

6.

7.

8.

Tré Rodriguez

9.

10.

11.

12.

13.

14.

15.

The 30 Day Job Search Survival Guide

In the next table spend some time writing your ideal answers to these questions. When you're writing your answers, keep in mind that you want to be sure you answer the question in a way that will be both relevant and interesting to your audience. If you can do this while telling a brief but engaging story that showcases your experience, even better!

Then find someone who can help you with some mock interview practice. You might choose someone on your network support team or you might choose someone you live with. For some of you who want that extra bit of help, you can hire a career counselor or coach to do a professional mock interview with you. Whichever strategy you select is fine, the important thing is to practice! Have the person who is helping you take notes. After you're done go over their feedback with them and brainstorm ways that you can improve your performance. Do this as many times as necessary to get fully comfortable.

Tré Rodriguez

> **Recruiter Tip:** If you have already put yourself to the test with answering likely questions, you will easily have your best responses on hand. It's like building muscle memory in sports. You don't want the first time you've encountered a likely interview question to be in the interview.

The 30 Day Job Search Survival Guide

Day 20
Potential Interview Question Answers

1.

2.

3.

4.

5.

6.

7.

8.

Tré Rodriguez

9.

10.

11.

12.

13.

14.

15.

The 30 Day Job Search Survival Guide

Day 21

Video Interview

"If a picture is worth a thousand words, how much is a video worth?"
David Kain

The last time I checked, it was reported that eighty percent of interviews were going to be held via video chat in the future. Even if that figure is exaggerated, it's no surprise that video interviews, because of their cost-effectiveness and the dispersed nature of the candidate pool, are becoming more common.

Some elements of preparing for a video interview are the same as preparing for an in-person interview. Yet you will need to consider some additional factors. Things that will matter are hardware, software, connection, time, screen area, audio, and privacy.

First, check your hardware. Is your computer in good working condition? Have you made sure that it is charged or that you have the cable available and plugged in? What about your headphones and microphone? Test them out the day before to make sure they are working. If they

Tré Rodriguez

aren't this will give you time to find alternatives. I generally recommend using headphones for interviews to ensure you can hear the interviewer(s) well.

   Which software will be needed, if any, to be interviewed? Will the company ask you to use an online meeting service? If so: test it out before! Make sure that you can log in. Normal interview etiquette is to show up at least ten minutes before the scheduled time. With video interviews, it's best to be sitting in front of your machine thirty minutes before so that you have time to resolve any technical difficulties that might arise.

   How is your internet connection? If your connection at home is inconsistent, plan to be at a place with a more stable connection on the day of your interview. Test it the morning of your scheduled date so that if anything has gone wrong, you'll have time to have it repaired or relocate without having to cancel.

   Depending on where the company is you might have a time difference. Make sure that when you write the appointment on your schedule that you factor in the time

The 30 Day Job Search Survival Guide

change! Few interviewers will be understanding about this kind of mix up.

At least a day before, set up your computer in the place you plan to conduct your interview. Sit at your machine and turn the camera on. Take a detailed and discriminating view of everything that appears in the screen area. This includes the background: walls, windows, bookshelves, beds, hallways, etc. Look at your screen through your potential interviewer's eyes. Would they be turned off by a poster hanging on the wall? Would they respond well to a messy room? What books or media are on your shelf, is there anything you would prefer they not see? Clean up your space or select a different place to sit if need be. Be sure to reassess the screen area if you move locations.

Where will you conduct your interview and what is the sound atmosphere like? Remember that your microphone tends to amplify every little noise. Therefore, it is best to choose the quietest and most peaceful location possible. If you have young children, arrange something so that the noise they make won't disturb you. If you or the neighbors are having construction done, pick a different location. Do

Tré Rodriguez

not interview in a public cafe or restaurant if you can help it because the noise will be unpredictable and typically beyond your control.

    Which brings us to our final concern: privacy. You need to block off at least an hour, unless notified ahead that it will be longer, in which you will not be disturbed, save for emergencies. This is not the time to be taking phone calls, or for someone to step into the room and ask you where you put the thing-a-ma-bob. Make sure the people around you know that it is critical they give you this time to focus. Lock the door if you can.

The 30 Day Job Search Survival Guide

Day 21
Video Interview Preparation Checklist

1.	Ensure all hardware is functioning properly.	
2.	Locate and test the necessary software.	
3.	Verify a reliable internet connection.	
4.	Confirm appointment date and time-zone.	
5.	Test and review screen area with a camera.	
6.	Arrange a quiet atmosphere for good audio.	
7.	Negotiate uninterrupted time for privacy.	

Tré Rodriguez

Day 22

Confront Your Bias

*"We see the world not as it is,
but as we are."*
Stephen R. Covey

It is an unfortunate truth that there is discrimination in hiring. The playing field is far from level. There are mountains of studies and anecdotal stories that show this. The adage, "twice as good to get half as much credit," still proves true for many.

I also want to make it clear that there are systemic biases against particular groups that limit access to opportunities to enter and advance in the working ecosystem. It is important that these system failures be rectified for the benefit of the working community at large and to enable our society to utilize all of the talent available. I advocate that we all take an active role in ways big and small over the long term to improve this situation and have done so since 2012 when I started my consulting business.

The 30 Day Job Search Survival Guide

That said, I can't tell you how many times I have heard stories where a candidate or individual thought that discrimination was going on and… it wasn't. Or when someone assumed that an individual was biased against a certain group… and they weren't.

That is why it is so incredibly important that we do not make assumptions or project our perspectives onto the people we come into contact with throughout the hiring process.

My clients come from all ages, classes, genders, a variety of ethnicities, and backgrounds and so do the people interviewing them. Recently a few clients of mine expressed that they were very concerned about age bias — they were all over 50 years old. However, upon further probing, I uncovered that they were biased against the people interviewing them because of their youth! They were projecting their preoccupation about age onto the interviewers, who may or may not have held the same opinion.

You might come into contact with a white man who is a champion of young women of color. You might interview

Tré Rodriguez

with a middle-aged woman who is biased against other women. You might engage with a black man who has no preference regarding employee's identities as long as they are good at Math. You might interact with a young Latino founder who is dying to hire an advisor who is older than she is and can share their wisdom and experience. People can sometimes surprise us.

So many things play into the biases that each of us hold and few, if any, of us can honestly claim that we have no prejudices or preferences. Yet to assume that a person holds an opinion based on their membership of a certain identity group is not only unfair, it is strategically unsound.

If you encounter systemic or blatant discrimination, it is important that you think carefully and calmly about how to address it. Depending on the situation, you may have a variety of options that include doing nothing all the way up to calling the cops, reporting the business, filing a lawsuit, or making a formal complaint through the appropriate channels. It is not the goal of this guide to give legal advice. My caution here is to weigh your options thoughtfully and make the choice that your conscience can live with. If you aren't sure about your particular situation it

The 30 Day Job Search Survival Guide

may be a good idea to get feedback from a mentor, friend, colleague, career coach, or employment lawyer that you trust. Don't feel rushed to action! It's OK to take time to consider your options while prioritizing your mental, physical, and emotional safety. In the long run, you will be happy to have approached the matter with a cool head.

Throughout my career I have been discriminated against various times. I'd say that a low estimate would be that I have experienced one event for every job I've held and, in many cases, it was much more. Each experience warranted a different response depending on the unique factors of my position. When choosing companies to partner with it has been my preference to avoid those that are biased against me in favor for those that embrace my specific set of qualities. Others prefer to challenge systems and become the first or the one that gets through. This is not my style and I have opted to use my energies elsewhere.

If the situation is uncertain, before you write someone off as prejudiced against you, take a moment for introspection. Ask yourself if you might be judging them

Tré Rodriguez

unfairly. You might not be. Still, it's worth considering as a safeguard anyway.

To become aware of your potential biases, fill out the table on the next sheet. The first column is for your identities. An identity is a primary, defining characteristic of who you are. For example, woman/man, Native American/European/African American, immigrant, straight/gay/lesbian, etc. In the next table, imagine what preferences or prejudices someone with these identities might hold. Now it doesn't mean that you hold them. At this stage, we are just imagining. This exercise will help you to remain open-minded and self-aware.

The 30 Day Job Search Survival Guide

Day 22
Confront Your Bias

My Identities	Preferences or Prejudices That Are Possible to Hold Related to These Indentities

Tré Rodriguez

Day 23
Turn the Tables

An interview is a two-way street.

Something that many job seekers forget is that an interview is a two-way street. As much as an employer is trying to see if you would be a good addition to their team, you are also checking them out to see if you would enjoy working with them. Your skills, your expertise, and the pleasure of your company are valuable assets that should be shared with those whom you determine deserving.

Therefore, you need to be prepared to evaluate the company and people you come into contact with during your interview. This is especially true when you've been dreaming about a specific company for some time. Be open to the possibility that it may look different from the inside than the outside.

When you walk in, notice the environment. Does the office have a lot of light? How is the air? Do they have windows, patios, plants, or access to an area with nature?

The 30 Day Job Search Survival Guide

Are the employees sitting in cubicles, in offices, or do they have an open office plan? How are the desks and chairs? Do they look comfortable? Are the working areas clean, messy, formal, or informal?

How are the employees dressed? Do they look comfortable or highly polished? Would you like to dress the same way for a year or more? Are they working in groups or individually? Look at their faces and listen to the tones of their voices. Do they seem happy, relaxed, or stressed out? You can tell a lot about a working environment and corporate culture by paying attention to these kinds of details.

When you are meeting your interviewers, how do they approach you? Are they friendly, neutral, or aggressive? Do they seem enthusiastic, bored, or harried? Is your conversation with them easy or does it feel difficult? Do you think you would like to work with them daily?

Hopefully, you will have an opportunity to meet your potential boss. If this is not offered to you, be sure to ask if you can! The single most important person in your working experience is your direct boss. See if you have anything in common. Do you feel comfortable talking with this person?

Tré Rodriguez

Are they interested in you, or just in what you can do for them? Feel free to ask about the career progress of people who have worked for them before. If those people have gone on, supported by this boss, to do bigger and better things that is a good sign! If they are all still there or have chosen to quit or transfer away from that boss, proceed with caution. To the best of your ability, see if you can determine if your potential boss is supportive or competitive. You don't need someone who is going to be holding you down or taking credit for your work.

As soon as you finish an interview, make a page of notes about your impressions of the company as a whole, the office, and each person you met. Keep these on file for when you are considering or comparing offers. Don't rely on your memory. Write things down.

When you are given the opportunity to ask questions, do not waste it! This is an important time to show the level of your knowledge about them and convey your genuine interest in the company and role. If you ask nothing or ask generic questions, your interviewers will think that you are not that interested in working for them or that you are lazy. If you ask interesting, genuine questions you can leave a

The 30 Day Job Search Survival Guide

great impression and gain valuable information to inform your next steps.

What some of you may like about a company others will hate and that's fine. When you are noticing all of these things you are not looking for an exact right or wrong answer, you are looking for what suits you best.

Tré Rodriguez

> **Recruiter Tip:** One great question to ask the person interviewing you is, what is their favorite aspect of working for that company or within that group? You want to subtly give them the idea that you are comparing their opportunity with others, and give them the chance to compete as the most attractive employer. It's an easy way to project confidence while keeping the interview conversational.

Spend some time today researching follow-up questions for an interview. Make a list of five questions you might ask here.

The 30 Day Job Search Survival Guide

Day 23
Interview Follow-Up Questions

1.

2.

3.

4.

5.

Tré Rodriguez

Day 24
Say Thank You!

"Anyone too busy to say thank you will get fewer and fewer chances to say it."
Harvey MacKay

Who doesn't like being appreciated for their time and effort? The practice of saying thank you to interviewers is going out of style. This is unfortunate because it's the polite thing to do. Fortunately for you, since people aren't doing it as much, it's an easy way for you to stand out. How and when you say thank you is something to consider thoughtfully.

If someone gave you a simple, "thanks!" after you did something for them, you would feel nice. If someone told you, "Thank you, I really appreciate that you took time out of your busy schedule to speak with me," you would likely feel appreciated and recognized for your efforts.

If someone said, "Thank you for spending your limited time with me. I know you have many things to do and so I recognize your efforts. I especially enjoyed our conversation about intergalactic time travel. By the way, did you know there's an intergalactic time travel conference in our area next Wednesday? I just thought I'd mention it. Thank you again and I look forward to hearing back from you about my candidacy." Now this person has your attention!

As with most things, the more thought and effort you put into saying thank you the better it will be received. Make it personal and genuine.

If it's possible, a handwritten note on stationery delivered within a day or two of your interview can go over well. A well-written email can also work. Whichever method you choose, you should send thank-you notes to everyone you spoke with during your interview process. This includes the receptionist or administrative assistant! Do not underestimate the power and influence these gatekeepers often have. If you end up getting an offer and accept, you will be grateful for having started your connection with your future coworkers on the right foot.

Tré Rodriguez

> **Recruiter Tip:** In the tech world, a prompt email a couple of hours after the interview is best. If it's a fast-paced environment, you want to show that you have a sense of urgency.

Make a list of people to thank. Include anyone who has helped you in any way so far and all people you have come into contact with at your desired companies. Update this list throughout your job search to be sure you haven't forgotten anyone.

The 30 Day Job Search Survival Guide

Day 24
Thank You Note Checklist

	Person to Thank	Company or Association	Email	X
1.				
2.				
3.				
4.				
5.				
6.				
7.				
8.				
9.				
10.				
11.	+			

Tré Rodriguez

Day 25

Prepare for the Salary Negotiation

"In business, as in life, you don't get what you deserve. You get what you negotiate."
Chester L. Karrass

In a perfect world, all jobs would be paid fairly and all employees would earn exactly what they are worth. Unfortunately, the world is far from perfect and for that, we have the salary negotiation.

If you look at a hiring decision from a business or purchase perspective, this makes a lot of sense. When you go to the store you want to maximize the value you can get while paying as little as possible. If you are looking at a pair of off-brand shoes, you are willing to pay a certain amount. If suddenly those are name brand shoes, which implies higher quality and therefore longer durability and performance, you might be convinced to pay more. You exchange more money for a higher value. If you find out that all of the stores in your geographic area are selling these name brand shoes for about the same price, you become more comfortable with paying that price. The more relevant and useful features the shoes have, the

The 30 Day Job Search Survival Guide

more you are willing to pay. If those features exist but you don't know about them, you won't pay more for them. If a salesperson is informing you of them, you will.

This thought experiment works better if you pretend that the internet and Amazon don't exist. But don't think they aren't relevant! The internet and remote workers are exactly one of the reasons competition is getting so stiff. Employers can hire equally, or better, qualified workers who have a lower cost of living in a different location and pay them less. That's the equivalent of you buying your Nikes online instead of at the local strip mall.

Your goal today is to research the going salary range for the job titles you identified in your ideal job profile on day four. Make sure that the data you collect is specific for zip code, years of experience, education, number of direct reports, company size, and industry.

If you find that you can't, or don't want to, do this research yourself you can hire a career counselor or coach to create a custom salary report for you. The most important thing is to go into a negotiation knowing what the market rate is for your profession and industry so that you

Tré Rodriguez

can advocate for yourself from an informed place. In this case, knowledge truly is power. So always know your worth and always check the salary range.

> **Recruiter Tip:** New law in California as of 2018 — companies must disclose the budgeted salary range for any given position. This was passed to stop gender-based wage gaps. Previously, women who were being paid less for their job would have this problem throughout their entire career, as each subsequent job would ask their current salary and base their offer on that information, rather than on the market rate for their role. All companies in California or working with candidates in the state of California must comply. Additionally, many companies in other states are now operating in accordance with the California law.

The 30 Day Job Search Survival Guide

Day 25
Salary Research List

	Job Title	Industry	Salary Range
1.			
2.			
3.			
4.			
5.			
6.			
7.			
8.			

Tré Rodriguez

Day 26

Prepare for the Counter Offer

Each party should gain from a negotiation.

So, you've submitted your application, you've made it through a series of interviews, and you've landed a job offer. Congratulations! Take a minute to reflect on your progress and appreciate your achievement.

Now just because you've received an offer doesn't mean that your only options are to accept or reject. There is still room for negotiation to make sure that both parties enter into a relationship that feels fair and beneficial to both sides.

Also, don't feel down if your offer hasn't come exactly twenty-six days after you started this process. There are so many variables that factor into the hiring decision that for some people this will come sooner and for others, much later. Do not take this as a reflection of your worth as a candidate! Many of these variables will be outside of your control. Your job is to do your absolute best and prepare as much as you can.

The 30 Day Job Search Survival Guide

If, while comparing the salary research you completed earlier, you notice that the salary you have been offered is not within industry standards, don't despair just yet! Sometimes companies are not aware of what the going rate is. If you politely inform them that their offer is not within the market range, many companies will do the right thing and adjust their offer. If this is the case, you will be glad that you mentioned it and delayed feeling offended.

Sometimes a company will legitimately not have the budget to pay you more, but they can offer additional perks that would essentially make up the difference. For example, tuition reimbursement, remote working options, childcare, tax savings plans, health care savings accounts, or paid professional development via online courses or conferences. Make a list of additional compensation items that you would like to see in your package, or that would mean more to you than just an increase in money. If you can't think of what you might ask for, now is the time to do some internet research and ask around to find out what kind of things other companies have done.

Tré Rodriguez

When you determine what you think is fair and reasonable, research online to find out what the most recent style for counter offer letters are in your industry and geographic area. Write your letter and run it past a trusted mentor or friend and discuss what they think before you send it. If you feel more comfortable, you can also check in with a coach or career counselor.

Once you feel confident submit your letter to the company stressing how much you appreciate their offer and look forward to coming to a mutually beneficial arrangement that will allow both of you to start off on a great foot.

The 30 Day Job Search Survival Guide

Day 26
Alternative Compensation

	Non-Monetary Compensation Items That I Would Value
1.	
2.	
3.	
4.	
5.	
6.	
7.	
8.	
9.	
10.	
11.	
12.	
13.	
14.	
15.	

Tré Rodriguez

Counter Offer Feedback Tracking

Cover Letter	Feedback From	Comments Made	X When Feedback Integrated
1.			
2.			
3.			
4.			

The 30 Day Job Search Survival Guide

Day 27

Professional Organizations & Certifications

*"The rise or fall, success or failure of your dreams is largely dependent on
the association you build yourself around."*
Israelmore Ayivor

> **Covid-19 Adaptation**: if you are using this guide during Covid-19 or another situation that does not allow you to physically gather socially, think of ways that you can adapt your interactions. Can you use the phone, video conferencing, chat groups or other tools to achieve similar goals?

Joining professional organizations related to your industry, profession, or alma matter will give you access to people and information that you might not otherwise get. If the organizations you choose have periodic meet-ups, be sure to go! This could be a great networking opportunity and provide you with leads on open positions or changing industry trends. You can join the organization's group on LinkedIn to hear about job opportunities as well. Some individuals will make it a special point to post jobs to their associated groups. I know of at least one recruiter who specifically shares opportunities with our alum group

Tré Rodriguez

whenever she gets the opportunity. Be sure to join the listserve and subscribe to their updates as well.

Make a list of four professional organizations that you would consider joining here.

Professional Organizations

1.
2.
3.
4.

The 30 Day Job Search Survival Guide

Certifications can be an efficient, cost-effective, and schedule-friendly way to update your skills. Certification will cost less than a degree and will generally be more specific. If you are looking to add just a little bit more oomph to your application, this could be a great option for you.

Additionally, some industries expect or respect particular certificates. Some will require a certificate as part of the qualifying process. Therefore, this can be the best use of the extra time we usually have during a job search.

Research what types of certificates, if any, are available in your industry or profession. Look at the organizations that offer them, the time required to complete them, and any associated costs. Then, if it makes sense, choose one and go for it.

List at least three certificates that would be relevant to your situation.

Tré Rodriguez

Certifications

	Certificate Name	Institution or Organization	Time Required	Cost
1.				
2.				
3.				

The 30 Day Job Search Survival Guide

Day 28

Relocation

"We keep moving forward, opening new doors, and doing new things, because we are curious and our curiosity keeps leading us down new paths."
Walt Disney

As I mentioned in the first chapter, looking for a job or changing jobs can be one of the most stressful events of a person's life. One of the others? Moving. If you happen to be changing jobs and moving, you're carrying a heavier load. That means it's extra important to pay attention to things you can do to make the process go more smoothly.

First off, you have to decide if you are open to relocation as a result of your job search. Do your circumstances allow or require you to move for work? Take some time to review your situation, consider your options, and consider what alternatives you might have. This is a time when talking to an objective third party could be beneficial. Any of the people who are closely involved with you will have their reasons for why you should or should not relocate, and not all of them will necessarily consider your well-being as the priority.

Tré Rodriguez

If you do decide that relocating is your best option, the next thing you need to do is determine the details of where you would be willing to go and how you will get there. Some locations will be a better match than others. Some you would only consider if the compensation, opportunity, or timing was just right. What are your needs regarding the place where you would move? What things are must-haves, nice-to-haves, and really-don't-wants? What about the terms? Would you need a salary increase, a moving allowance, or more vacation time? Make some lists.

Then, spend some time reflecting on the lists you made. When you are reviewing an offer or going for an opportunity, check-in to see how well it matches your stated preferences.

The 30 Day Job Search Survival Guide

Day 28
Reasons to Relocate

Pros	Cons

Tré Rodriguez

Day 28
About Relocation City, State, or Country

Must Have	Nice to Have	Do Not Want

Relocation Terms

Must Have	Nice to Have	Do Not Want

The 30 Day Job Search Survival Guide

Day 29
You Got Fired or Laid Off

"Temporary setbacks are overshadowed by persistence."
Quentin L. Cook

Getting fired or laid off can be a devastating experience. What can make it worse is not managing the process of recovery. As with any traumatic event, there's some baggage to be dealt with.

When clients come to me after this experience they are often in shock. For some, their self-esteem has taken a huge blow. They might be in denial. Others feel pressure to bounce back immediately. Being fired or laid off can make you feel lost and disoriented, as though the rug has been pulled out from under you.

In addition to the emotional experience, being fired or laid off can cause financial and logistical problems. It might even cause relationship problems. It's important to not underestimate the varying consequences and take proactive steps to ensure that you survive the fallout.

Tré Rodriguez

As intense and shocking as receiving this news can be, the important thing is not to take any hasty actions. Don't write any mass emails, make any emotional phone calls, and don't publish any dramatic posts. When you contact someone, and you should contact someone, make sure that it's a person you can trust to be supportive. If you don't have anyone like that, it wouldn't be unwise to make an appointment with a career coach, behavioral counselor, or some other professional that can provide support.

It can be extremely difficult for people to remain calm and objective after being fired or laid off. The important thing is to get yourself into a supportive atmosphere. Take some time to process what has just happened to you. This might mean not going directly home and announcing the loss to the people in your immediate family who will be affected if their reaction will be an additional trauma. Many times, people will reach for unhealthy coping habits — drugs, alcohol, etc. — when something traumatic happens. It's important to resist this urge if you have it and to reach for healthier ways to cope. Review the list you made on day one for ideas.

The 30 Day Job Search Survival Guide

Once you've had some time to just sit with the event, take practical steps to address the other challenges. Assess your financial situation to figure out how much runway you have until you will be in trouble. If you need to and have access to one, contact a financial advisor. The company may have given you information about a severance package, unemployment, or out-placement services. Review this material thoroughly to figure out what kind of support you get. Review the unemployment office's page for your city or state and see what additional support you might find there. If you attended a university, contact their career services and see how they might be able to help.

Something important to remember: action kills anxiety and depression. When you are struggling, take whatever first step you can towards a resolution, then take the next one and then the next. You don't have to see the whole path all at once. All you need to do is keep taking small steps in the direction you think you want to go. As you progress you will learn more and adapt your decisions to your wider perspective. Even if you take a misstep or two you can double back and correct. This is how all of the

Tré Rodriguez

great achievements have been made throughout history —
one persistent step at a time.

The 30 Day Job Search Survival Guide

Day 29
Laid Off or Fired Quick Start Resolution Check List

1.	Get yourself into a supportive or at least neutral atmosphere to process what just happened.	
2.	Contact a trusted person from your support network to share the news.	
3.	Assess your financial situation and the impact the event will have.	
4.	Review any literature or information that was provided during the letting go.	
5.	Review the city or state's unemployment website and become familiar with its resources.	
6.	If applicable, contact your alma mater(s) career services.	
7.	Create or follow a job search plan. For example, the 30 Day Job Search Survival Guide	

Tré Rodriguez

Day 30
Final Review

"Discipline is the bridge between goals and accomplishment."
Jim Rohn

Congratulations! You have made it through the entire 30 Day Job Search Survival Guide. I applaud you for your commitment and discipline. I appreciate your allowing me to ride along this journey with you. I am very grateful that my experiences have given me the knowledge and information to smooth the path for others so that you can benefit from the lessons I learned the hard way.

As I mentioned before, this system works as well as you work the process. Some people will just skim this guide, some people will read it with attention and detail. Other people will carefully and thoughtfully complete all of the exercises. Generally, the people who have the most success will complete a thorough reading and working of the guide. Not just once, but several times, with each time getting better and more focused than the last.

The 30 Day Job Search Survival Guide

One of the most important characteristics of any successful job search is accountability. Accountability matters more in job searching than in many other arenas in life because no boss is standing over you to enforce it. You are your own boss and your results are the marker of how good a boss you are. In a job search, not everything is within your control which is why it is so important that you manage the parts that are. Being accountable and taking disciplined action is a learnable habit that gets easier with practice. It's important that you honestly evaluate your efforts up until now. Consider how they can be improved and made more effective. To do so, answer the following questions as completely and honestly as possible.

Tré Rodriguez

Day 30
General Questions

	Question	Your comments
1.	What has gone well during my job search? Why has it gone well?	
2.	What success have I had? What contributed to that success?	
3.	What has not gone so well during my job search? Why has it not gone so well?	
4.	Have I had any failures? What can I learn from my failures? What can I do to increase the likelihood of my succeeding next time I try?	

The 30 Day Job Search Survival Guide

Specific Questions

Ch.	Topic	Question	Your Comments & Adjustments
1.	*Do Nothing*	Are the activities that you chose supporting you in staying calm and happy? If not, what can you change to make them more effective?	
2.	*Set Up a Routine*	Have you been keeping your routine? Does it help? If not, what adjustments can you make to improve it?	
3.	*Build Your Team*	Are the people on your list available and supportive? Have you called on them and received satisfactory responses? If not, do you need to add or subtract people, or change your approach?	

Tré Rodriguez

4.	*Ideal Job Profile*	It's time to update your Ideal Job Profile with the new information you've learned or identified through this process. What has changed or become more specific for you?	
5.	*Informational Interview*	Have you been able to conduct at least one informational interview? If not, why not? What can you do to ensure that you are taking this valuable step to gather information?	
6.	*Resume*	Have you updated your resume? Did you ask anyone for feedback? Did you make improvements based on their commentary? If not, how can you move forward on this step?	

The 30 Day Job Search Survival Guide

7.	*Get Active, Get Outdoors*	Have you been able to spend at least ten minutes per day outdoors? Does your list of activities need to be updated with items that will motivate you more? Could adding a partner to your activities help? How can you ensure this will happen?	
8.	*Cover Letter*	Did you make a least three cover letter drafts and get feedback on them from people you trust? If not, why not? What can you do to be sure that you are getting the CL practice you need?	
9.	*Google Yourself*	Did you Google yourself? Were the results satisfactory? If not, what actions have you taken to improve them?	

Tré Rodriguez

10.	*LinkedIn Profile*	How does your LinkedIn profile look? Did you spend at least eight hours updating it, making sure that it is complete and polished as possible? If not, why not?	
11.	*Personal Website*	Have you made at least a simple personal website to improve your search results and online presence? If not, what is holding you back? What can you do today to start the process?	
12.	*Ask for Help*	Have you sent an email to all of your contacts asking for support? If yes, what were the results? Have you followed-up on any offered help?	

The 30 Day Job Search Survival Guide

13.	*Actual Job Searching*	How is your job searching going? How often are you applying to jobs? Are you reaching at least a 30% return rate on resumes submitted? If not, what can you do to improve your return rate?	
14.	*Give Back*	Have you identified ten people, groups, or organizations that are in need of your help? Have you contributed in some way, however small, to at least one of them? If not, why not?	
15.	*Recruiters & Staffing Agencies*	Have you contacted at least one staffing agency or recruiter? If not, why not?	

Tré Rodriguez

16.	*Check-In*	Did you complete the check-in from Chapter 16? Did it help you refine your job searching actions? If yes, how? If no, why not?	
17.	*Get Social*	Have you been participating in at least one social activity since you started reading this guide? Why or why not? What can you do to increase your likelihood to do so?	
18.	*Developing Yourself*	Have you undertaken steps to continue your self-development? What did you do and how did it go? If you haven't, what barrier is holding you back and how can you remove it?	

The 30 Day Job Search Survival Guide

19.	Read	Have you been reading at least ten pages per day? What have you read and what have you gained from the experience? If you haven't, why not?	
20.	Interview Skills	Have you worked to improve your interview skills? What impact has this had on your confidence and comfort level? If you haven't, what has stopped you?	
21.	Video Interview	Have you worked through the video interview checklist? If not, why not?	

Tré Rodriguez

22.	*Confront Your Bias*	Have you spent any time considering the conscious and unconscious biases you might hold regarding your job search? How has this helped you to be more objective? If you haven't, why not?	
23.	*Turn the Tables*	Have you thought about the characteristics that you are looking for in your ideal job? Have you drafted a list of questions you can ask an inteviewer?	
25.	*Salary Negotiation*	Have you done your research so that you know the market rate for your profession and industry? Has this increased your confidence when you consider negotiating your value? If you haven't, why not?	

The 30 Day Job Search Survival Guide

26.	*Counter Offer*	Have you spent some time considering what non-monetary compensation you would appreciate? If not, why not?	
27.	*Organizations & Certifications*	Have you done any research to find out what professional organizations or certifications would be beneficial to you in your profession and industry? If yes, have you taken steps to join an organization or begin a certification? If not, why not?	
28.	*Relocation*	Have you considered whether or not relocation is an option for you and under what circumstances you would agree to it? If not, why not?	

Tré Rodriguez

29.	*Fired or Laid Off*	If you have not been fired or laid off, your only goal here is to do the thought experiment of what would happen if you were. Take a few minutes and reflect about the steps you would take.	
30.	*Final Review*	Did you complete the final review? Was it insightful to consider your engagement in the process? How did you benefit from keeping yourself accountable, if at all? If not, why not?	

The 30 Day Job Search Survival Guide

Afterward

I know some of you will have gotten this far without having done any of the exercises. You might have asked yourself throughout the chapters why I didn't just give you the answers to some of them or a list of resources to find them. You'll say you didn't have the time or that you got the main point or intention behind the idea so you don't need to write anything down or do any research. That is one option of how to use this guide.

May I explain why I suggest a better option? Learning is more than just reading. Learning is doing. Learning is searching. Some studies show that the more effort you put into acquiring information, the better you will integrate it. Superior integration translates to useable knowledge at the critical moments of life. I don't want you to just kind of get how to do a job search. I want you to become anti-fragile when it comes to job searching. Have you heard the term anti-fragile? If you haven't, you've probably heard of the term resilient. Resilient people bounce back from setbacks or crises. Anti-fragile people become better as a result of the set back or crisis. My wish for you is that for every job search you go through you come out better than before.

So, if you haven't yet done the exercises, consider spending some time on them. Maybe you will even consider doing them

Tré Rodriguez

as many times as needed until job searches don't worry you, they excite you with the possibilities!

Thank you for allowing me to share some of the wisdom I've gained throughout the years. If the things I have learned can make your life more efficient and fruitful, I will feel grateful and satisfied.

Again, if you find the material in this book useful, I would appreciate it if you could take a minute or two to leave a review on Amazon.com, Goodreads.com, or whichever site you purchased the book from and use to track your reading. This helps more people find this information. Thank you!

I wish you so much success and happiness.

Good luck and happy searching.

The 30 Day Job Search Survival Guide

Appendix A - Resources

When I chose to create this guide, it was critically important to have input from the best and the brightest working in order to provide the absolute highest quality to my audience. Therefore, I am happy to recommend my contributors with absolutely no reservations whatsoever.

April Starlight
Owner and Recruiter, Tangerine Search Inc., San Francisco
www.linkedin.com/in/aprilstarlight
www.tangerinesearch.net

Deborah Gavrin Frangquist
Career Counseling, Executive Coach, Chosen Futures, San Francisco
www.linkedin.com/in/deborahgfrangquist

Sandy Cruze
Former Manager of Google, Oracle, eBay, Sun Microsystems, and Former Executive at Risk Management Solutions and Alaska Tribal Health Consortium, San Francisco
www.linkedin.com/in/sandracruze

Nick Martinez
Strategic Marketing, Albuquerque
www.linkedin.com/in/nicholasmtz
www.nicholasmtz.com

Anna Stein
Editor, Seattle

Tré Rodriguez

Appendix B - Extra tables

To facilitate your reusing this guide I have provided you with two extra copies of the tables from each chapter.

The 30 Day Job Search Survival Guide

Day 1
10 Feel Good Activities

1.	6.
2.	7.
3.	8.
4.	9.
5.	10.

Tré Rodriguez

Day 2
Daily Routine

1.	6.
2.	7.
3.	8.
4.	9.
5.	10.

The 30 Day Job Search Survival Guide

Day 3
Support Network

	Name	Number	Email
1.			
2.			
3.			
4.			
5.			

Tré Rodriguez

Day 4
Ideal Job Profile

Location:	Working on a team or working individually
Company size: big, medium, small	Working on-site, remotely, or a combination
Industry:	Liberal or conservative company culture
Type of service or product:	Identity group friendly, i.e LGBTQ, African American, immigrants, etc.
Job Title(s):	Leadership profile that includes specific charactertistics, i.e. women, minorities, certain age groups, etc.
Reputation for something specific, i.e. giving back to the community, innovation, child-friendly, etc.	Other
Other	Other

The 30 Day Job Search Survival Guide

Day 5
Informational Interview Questions

1.

2.

3.

4.

5.

6.

Tré Rodriguez

7.

8.

9.

10.

The 30 Day Job Search Survival Guide

Day 7
Outdoor Activities

> **Covid-19 Adaptation**: if you are using this guide during Covid-19 or another situation that does not allow you to physically gather socially, think of ways that you can adapt your interactions to follow the most recent safety requirements provided by your local authorities.

1.

2.

3.

4.

5.

Tré Rodriguez

Day 8
Cover Letter Feedback Tracking

Cover Letter	Feedback From	Comments Made	X When Feedback Integrated
1.			
2.			
3.			
4.			

The 30 Day Job Search Survival Guide

Day 10
Quick Start LinkedIn Profile Checklist

1.	Relevant or interesting cover photo	
2.	Excellent profile photo	
3.	Well written, first-person summary	
4.	Complete work history that addresses work gaps	
5.	Complete education section including honors	
6.	Organization memberships	
7.	Certificates	
8.	In-demand skills for endorsing	
9.	Customized profile link	
10.	Relevant profile heading	
11.	Interesting or relevant projects	
12.	Interesting or relevant coursework	
13.	Recommendations from colleagues, bosses, or clients	

Tré Rodriguez

Day 11
Personal Websites I Like

	Address	What I Like
1.		
2.		
3.		

Use this checklist to get started. This is in not meant to be an exhaustive list.

Personal Website Checklist

1.	Website address:	
2.	Your name as listed on your resume, LinkedIn, etc.	
3.	Your photo – if using	
4.	Your education and training	
5.	Your preferred job title(s) and industry(ies)	
6.	Your resume in PDF	
7.	List of your top skills	
8.	Recommendations for your work	
9.	Examples of your work, if able	
10.	Links to your relevant social media	
11.	Links to relevant content owned by you	
12.	Links to relevant content not owned by you	

The 30 Day Job Search Survival Guide

Day 12
Asking for Help Check List

1.	Gather contacts from:	
	K-12	
	college or university if attended	
	previous jobs	
	community connections	
	family	
	any other social contacts	
2.	Draft an email using the example above	
3.	Complete email using information from ideal job profile	
4.	Send email in batches grouped by relevance	
5.	Select day to follow-up with contacts	
6.	Follow-up	
7.	Record any leads and follow them	
8.	Say thank you to anyone who provided help	
9.	Say thank you to anyone who provided encouragement	

Tré Rodriguez

Day 13
Job Search Action Plan Check List

1.	Research and apply to the _____ company	
2.	Review _____ website completely	
3.	Search for latest news dealing with _____	
4.	Search and study at least 10 _____ employees on LinkedIn in the area of interest to see what their background is	
5.	Search to see if I have any contacts at _____ that can make me an introduction	
6.	Try to get an informational interview with someone who works or has worked at _____ and ask them questions about culture, fit, and working environment — do not ask them for help getting a job	
7.	Find two of the best-fit job postings at _____	
8.	Tailor resume to _____ style	
9.	Tailor cover letter to _____ specific details	
10.		
11.		
12.		
13.		
14.		

The 30 Day Job Search Survival Guide

Day 14
Paying It Forward List

Person, family, or group	What they need	How I can help
1.		
2.		
3.		
4.		
5.		
6.		
7.		
8.		
9.		
10.		

Tré Rodriguez

Day 15
Recruiter and Staffing Agency Contact List

Found via	Company	Contact	Email / Phone	Follow Up	Follow Up	Follow Up

The 30 Day Job Search Survival Guide

Day 16
Halfway Check-In Accountability Questionnaire

Ch.	Topic	Question	Your Comments & Adjustments
1.	*Do Nothing*	Are the activities that you chose supporting you in staying calm and happy? If not, what can you change to make them more effective?	
2.	*Set-Up a Routine*	Have you been keeping your routine? Does it help? If not, what adjustments can you make that will work better?	

Tré Rodriguez

3.	*Build Your Team*	Are the people on your list available and supportive? Have you called on them and received satisfactory responses? If not, do you need to adjust your list or change your approach?	
4.	*Ideal Job Profile*	It's time to update your ideal job profile with the new information you've learned or identified through this process. What has changed or become more specific for you?	
5.	*Informational Interview*	Have you been able to conduct at least one informational interview? If not, why not? What can you do to ensure that you are taking this valuable step? If you have conducted interview(s), what have you learned?	

The 30 Day Job Search Survival Guide

6.	*Resume*	Have you updated your resume? Did you ask anyone for feedback and did you make improvements based on their commentary? If not, what can you do to move forward?	
7.	*Get Active, Get Outdoors*	Have you been able to spend at least 10 minutes per day outdoors? If not, why not? Does your list of activities need to be updated with items that will motivate you more? Could adding a partner to your activities help? How can you ensure this will happen?	

Tré Rodriguez

8.	*Cover Letter*	Did you make at least three cover letter drafts and get feedback on them from people you trust? If not, why not? What can you do to be sure that you are getting the CL practice you need?	
9.	*Google Yourself*	Did you Google yourself? Were the results satisfactory? If not, what actions have you taken to improve them?	
10.	*LinkedIn Profile*	How does your LinkedIn profile look? Did you spend at least eight hours updating it and making sure that it is complete and as polished as possible? If not, why not?	

The 30 Day Job Search Survival Guide

11.	*Personal Website*	Have you made a simple personal website to improve your search results and online presence? If not, what is holding you back? What can you do today to start the process?	
12.	*Ask for Help*	Have you sent an email to all of your contacts asking for support? If yes, what were the results? Have you followed up on any offered help? If no, what stopped you and how can you push past it?	
13.	*Actual Job Searching*	How is your job searching going? How often are you applying to jobs? Are you reaching at least a 30% return rate on resumes submitted? If not, what can you do to improve your return rate?	

Tré Rodriguez

14.	*Give Back*	Have you identified ten people, groups, or organizations that need your help? Have you contributed in some way, however small, to at least one of them? If not, why not?	
15.	*Recruiters & Staffing Agencies*	Have you contacted at least one staffing agency or recruiter? If not, why not?	

The 30 Day Job Search Survival Guide

Day 17
Social Activities

> **Covid-19 Adaptation**: if you are using this guide during Covid-19 or another situation that does not allow you to physically gather socially, think of ways that you can adapt your interactions. Can you use the phone, video conferencing, chat groups, or other tools to achieve similar goals?

Activity	Day + Time
1.	
2.	
3.	
4.	

Tré Rodriguez

Day 18
Most Wanted General Skills

1.	3.	5.
2.	4.	6.

Most Wanted Industry Skills

1.	3.	5.
2.	4.	6.

The 30 Day Job Search Survival Guide

Day 18
Skills I Want to Gain or Improve

1.	2.

How I Can Gain These Skills

1.	3.	5.
2.	4.	6.

Tré Rodriguez

Day 19
Reading List

1.	6.
2.	7.
3.	8.
4.	9.
5.	10.

The 30 Day Job Search Survival Guide

Day 20
Potential Interview Questions

1.

2.

3.

4.

5.

6.

7.

8.

Tré Rodriguez

9.

10.

11.

12.

13.

14.

15.

The 30 Day Job Search Survival Guide

Day 21
Video Interview Preparation Checklist

1.	Ensure all hardware is functioning properly.
2.	Locate and test the necessary software.
3.	Verify a reliable internet connection.
4.	Confirm appointment date and time-zone.
5.	Test and review screen area with a camera.
6.	Arrange a quiet atmosphere for good audio.
7.	Negotiate uninterrupted time for privacy.

Tré Rodriguez

Day 22
Confront Your Bias

My Identities	Preferences or Prejudices That Are Possible to Hold Related to These Indentities

The 30 Day Job Search Survival Guide

Day 23
Interview Follow-Up Questions

1.

2.

3.

4.

5.

Tré Rodriguez

Day 24
Thank You Note Checklist

	Person to Thank	Company or Association	Email	X
1.				
2.				
3.				
4.				
5.				
6.				
7.				
8.				
9.				
10.				
11.	+			

The 30 Day Job Search Survival Guide

Day 25
Salary Research List

	Job Title	Industry	Salary Range
1.			
2.			
3.			
4.			
5.			
6.			
7.			
8.			

Tré Rodriguez

Day 26
Alternative Compensation

	Non-Monetary Compensation Items That I Would Value
1.	
2.	
3.	
4.	
5.	
6.	
7.	
8.	
9.	
10.	
11.	
12.	
13.	
14.	
15.	

The 30 Day Job Search Survival Guide

Counter Offer Feedback Tracking

Cover Letter	Feedback From	Comments Made	X When Feedback Integrated
1.			
2.			
3.			
4.			

Tré Rodriguez

Day 27
Professional Organizations

1.
2.
3.
4.

The 30 Day Job Search Survival Guide

Day 28
Reasons to Relocate

Pros	Cons

Tré Rodriguez

Day 28
About Relocation City, State, or Country

Must Have	Nice to Have	Do Not Want

Relocation Terms

Must Have	Nice to Have	Do Not Want

The 30 Day Job Search Survival Guide

Day 29
Laid Off or Fired Quick Start Resolution Check List

1.	Get yourself into a supportive or at least neutral atmosphere to process what just happened.	
2.	Contact a trusted person from your support network to share the news.	
3.	Assess your financial situation and the impact the event will have.	
4.	Review any literature or information that was provided during the letting go.	
5.	Review the city or state's unemployment website and become familiar with its resources.	
6.	If applicable, contact your alma mater(s) career services.	
7.	Create or follow a job search plan. For example, the 30 Day Job Search Survival Guide	

Tré Rodriguez

Day 30
General Questions

	Question	Your comments
1.	What has gone well during my job search? Why has it gone well?	
2.	What success have I had? What contributed to that success?	
3.	What has not gone so well during my job search? Why has it not gone so well?	
4.	Have I had any failures? What can I learn from my failures? What can I do to increase the likelihood of my succeeding next time I try?	

The 30 Day Job Search Survival Guide

Specific Questions

Ch.	Topic	Question	Your Comments & Adjustments
1.	*Do Nothing*	Are the activities that you chose supporting you in staying calm and happy? If not, what can you change to make them more effective?	
2.	*Set Up a Routine*	Have you been keeping your routine? Does it help? If not, what adjustments can you make to improve it?	
3.	*Build Your Team*	Are the people on your list available and supportive? Have you called on them and received satisfactory responses? If not, do you need to add or subtract people, or change your approach?	

Tré Rodriguez

4.	*Ideal Job Profile*	It's time to update your Ideal Job Profile with the new information you've learned or identified through this process. What has changed or become more specific for you?	
5.	*Informational Interview*	Have you been able to conduct at least one informational interview? If not, why not? What can you do to ensure that you are taking this valuable step to gather information?	
6.	*Resume*	Have you updated your resume? Did you ask anyone for feedback? Did you make improvements based on their commentary? If not, how can you move forward on this step?	

The 30 Day Job Search Survival Guide

7.	*Get Active, Get Outdoors*	Have you been able to spend at least ten minutes per day outdoors? Does your list of activities need to be updated with items that will motivate you more? Could adding a partner to your activities help? How can you ensure this will happen?	
8.	*Cover Letter*	Did you make a least three cover letter drafts and get feedback on them from people you trust? If not, why not? What can you do to be sure that you are getting the CL practice you need?	
9.	*Google Yourself*	Did you Google yourself? Were the results satisfactory? If not, what actions have you taken to improve them?	

Tré Rodriguez

10.	LinkedIn Profile	How does your LinkedIn profile look? Did you spend at least eight hours updating it, making sure that it is complete and polished as possible? If not, why not?	
11.	Personal Website	Have you made at least a simple personal website to improve your search results and online presence? If not, what is holding you back? What can you do today to start the process?	
12.	Ask for Help	Have you sent an email to all of your contacts asking for support? If yes, what were the results? Have you followed-up on any offered help?	

The 30 Day Job Search Survival Guide

13.	Actual Job Searching	How is your job searching going? How often are you applying to jobs? Are you reaching at least a 30% return rate on resumes submitted? If not, what can you do to improve your return rate?	
14.	Give Back	Have you identified ten people, groups, or organizations that are in need of your help? Have you contributed in some way, however small, to at least one of them? If not, why not?	
15.	Recruiters & Staffing Agencies	Have you contacted at least one staffing agency or recruiter? If not, why not?	

Tré Rodriguez

16.	*Check-In*	Did you complete the check-in from Chapter 16? Did it help you refine your job searching actions? If yes, how? If no, why not?	
17.	*Get Social*	Have you been participating in at least one social activity since you started reading this guide? Why or why not? What can you do to increase your likelihood to do so?	
18.	*Developing Yourself*	Have you undertaken steps to continue your self-development? What did you do and how did it go? If you haven't, what barrier is holding you back and how can you remove it?	

The 30 Day Job Search Survival Guide

19.	*Read*	Have you been reading at least ten pages per day? What have you read and what have you gained from the experience? If you haven't, why not?	
20.	*Interview Skills*	Have you worked to improve your interview skills? What impact has this had on your confidence and comfort level? If you haven't, what has stopped you?	
21.	*Video Interview*	Have you worked through the video interview checklist? If not, why not?	

Tré Rodriguez

22.	Confront Your Bias	Have you spent any time considering the conscious and unconscious biases you might hold regarding your job search? How has this helped you to be more objective? If you haven't, why not?	
23.	Turn the Tables	Have you thought about the characteristics that you are looking for in your ideal job? Have you drafted a list of questions you can ask an inteviewer?	
25.	Salary Negotiation	Have you done your research so that you know the market rate for your profession and industry? Has this increased your confidence when you consider negotiating your value? If you haven't, why not?	

The 30 Day Job Search Survival Guide

26.	*Counter Offer*	Have you spent some time considering what non-monetary compensation you would appreciate? If not, why not?	
27.	*Organizations & Certifications*	Have you done any research to find out what professional organizations or certifications would be beneficial to you in your profession and industry? If yes, have you taken steps to join an organization or begin a certification? If not, why not?	
28.	*Relocation*	Have you considered whether or not relocation is an option for you and under what circumstances you would agree to it? If not, why not?	

Tré Rodriguez

29.	Fired or Laid Off	If you have not been fired or laid off, your only goal here is to do the thought experiment of what would happen if you were. Take a few minutes and reflect about the steps you would take.	
30.	Final Review	Did you complete the final review? Was it insightful to consider your engagement in the process? How did you benefit from keeping yourself accountable, if at all? If not, why not?	

The 30 Day Job Search Survival Guide

Day 1
10 Feel Good Activities

1.	6.
2.	7.
3.	8.
4.	9.
5.	10.

Tré Rodriguez

Day 2
Daily Routine

1.	6.
2.	7.
3.	8.
4.	9.
5.	10.

The 30 Day Job Search Survival Guide

Day 3
Support Network

	Name	Number	Email
1.			
2.			
3.			
4.			
5.			

Tré Rodriguez

Day 4
Ideal Job Profile

Location:	Working on a team or working individually
Company size: big, medium, small	Working on-site, remotely, or a combination
Industry:	Liberal or conservative company culture
Type of service or product:	Identity group friendly, i.e LGBTQ, African American, immigrants, etc.
Job Title(s) :	Leadership profile that includes specific charactertistics, i.e. women, minorities, certain age groups, etc.
Reputation for something specific, i.e. giving back to the community, innovation, child-friendly, etc.	Other
Other	Other

The 30 Day Job Search Survival Guide

Day 5
Informational Interview Questions

1.

2.

3.

4.

5.

6.

Tré Rodriguez

7.

8.

9.

10.

The 30 Day Job Search Survival Guide

Day 7
Outdoor Activities

> **Covid-19 Adaptation**: if you are using this guide during Covid-19 or another situation that does not allow you to physically gather socially, think of ways that you can adapt your interactions to follow the most recent safety requirements provided by your local authorities.

1.

2.

3.

4.

5.

Tré Rodriguez

Day 8
Cover Letter Feedback Tracking

Cover Letter	Feedback From	Comments Made	X When Feedback Integrated
1.			
2.			
3.			
4.			

The 30 Day Job Search Survival Guide

Day 10
Quick Start LinkedIn Profile Checklist

1.	Relevant or interesting cover photo	
2.	Excellent profile photo	
3.	Well written, first-person summary	
4.	Complete work history that addresses work gaps	
5.	Complete education section including honors	
6.	Organization memberships	
7.	Certificates	
8.	In-demand skills for endorsing	
9.	Customized profile link	
10.	Relevant profile heading	
11.	Interesting or relevant projects	
12.	Interesting or relevant coursework	
13.	Recommendations from colleagues, bosses, or clients	

Tré Rodriguez

Day 11
Personal Websites I Like

	Address	What I Like
1.		
2.		
3.		

Use this checklist to get started. This is in not meant to be an exhaustive list.

Personal Website Checklist

1.	Website address:	
2.	Your name as listed on your resume, LinkedIn, etc.	
3.	Your photo – if using	
4.	Your education and training	
5.	Your preferred job title(s) and industry(ies)	
6.	Your resume in PDF	
7.	List of your top skills	
8.	Recommendations for your work	
9.	Examples of your work, if able	
10.	Links to your relevant social media	
11.	Links to relevant content owned by you	
12.	Links to relevant content not owned by you	

The 30 Day Job Search Survival Guide

Day 12
Asking for Help Check List

1.	Gather contacts from:	
	K-12	
	college or university if attended	
	previous jobs	
	community connections	
	family	
	any other social contacts	
2.	Draft an email using the example above	
3.	Complete email using information from ideal job profile	
4.	Send email in batches grouped by relevance	
5.	Select day to follow-up with contacts	
6.	Follow-up	
7.	Record any leads and follow them	
8.	Say thank you to anyone who provided help	
9.	Say thank you to anyone who provided encouragement	

Tré Rodriguez

Day 13
Job Search Action Plan Check List

1.	Research and apply to the _____ company	
2.	Review _____ website completely	
3.	Search for latest news dealing with _____	
4.	Search and study at least 10 _____ employees on LinkedIn in the area of interest to see what their background is	
5.	Search to see if I have any contacts at _____ that can make me an introduction	
6.	Try to get an informational interview with someone who works or has worked at _____ and ask them questions about culture, fit, and working environment — do not ask them for help getting a job	
7.	Find two of the best-fit job postings at _____	
8.	Tailor resume to _____ style	
9.	Tailor cover letter to _____ specific details	
10.		
11.		
12.		
13.		
14.		

The 30 Day Job Search Survival Guide

Day 14
Paying It Forward List

Person, family, or group	What they need	How I can help
1.		
2.		
3.		
4.		
5.		
6.		
7.		
8.		
9.		
10.		

Tré Rodriguez

Day 15
Recruiter and Staffing Agency Contact List

Found via	Company	Contact	Email / Phone	Follow Up	Follow Up	Follow Up

The 30 Day Job Search Survival Guide

Day 16
Halfway Check-In Accountability Questionnaire

Ch.	Topic	Question	Your Comments & Adjustments
1.	*Do Nothing*	Are the activities that you chose supporting you in staying calm and happy? If not, what can you change to make them more effective?	
2.	*Set-Up a Routine*	Have you been keeping your routine? Does it help? If not, what adjustments can you make that will work better?	
3.	*Build Your Team*	Are the people on your list available and supportive? Have you called on them and received satisfactory responses? If not, do you need to adjust your list or change your approach?	

Tré Rodriguez

4.	*Ideal Job Profile*	It's time to update your ideal job profile with the new information you've learned or identified through this process. What has changed or become more specific for you?	
5.	*Information al Interview*	Have you been able to conduct at least one informational interview? If not, why not? What can you do to ensure that you are taking this valuable step? If you have conducted interview(s), what have you learned?	
6.	*Resume*	Have you updated your resume? Did you ask anyone for feedback and did you make improvements based on their commentary? If not, what can you do to move forward?	

The 30 Day Job Search Survival Guide

7.	*Get Active, Get Outdoors*	Have you been able to spend at least 10 minutes per day outdoors? If not, why not? Does your list of activities need to be updated with items that will motivate you more? Could adding a partner to your activities help? How can you ensure this will happen?	
8.	*Cover Letter*	Did you make at least three cover letter drafts and get feedback on them from people you trust? If not, why not? What can you do to be sure that you are getting the CL practice you need?	
9.	*Google Yourself*	Did you Google yourself? Were the results satisfactory? If not, what actions have you taken to improve them?	

Tré Rodriguez

10.	*LinkedIn Profile*	How does your LinkedIn profile look? Did you spend at least eight hours updating it and making sure that it is complete and as polished as possible? If not, why not?	
11.	*Personal Website*	Have you made a simple personal website to improve your search results and online presence? If not, what is holding you back? What can you do today to start the process?	
12.	*Ask for Help*	Have you sent an email to all of your contacts asking for support? If yes, what were the results? Have you followed up on any offered help? If no, what stopped you and how can you push past it?	

The 30 Day Job Search Survival Guide

13.	Actual Job Searching	How is your job searching going? How often are you applying to jobs? Are you reaching at least a 30% return rate on resumes submitted? If not, what can you do to improve your return rate?	
14.	Give Back	Have you identified ten people, groups, or organizations that need your help? Have you contributed in some way, however small, to at least one of them? If not, why not?	
15.	Recruiters & Staffing Agencies	Have you contacted at least one staffing agency or recruiter? If not, why not?	

Tré Rodriguez

Day 17
Social Activities

> **Covid-19 Adaptation**: if you are using this guide during Covid-19 or another situation that does not allow you to physically gather socially, think of ways that you can adapt your interactions. Can you use the phone, video conferencing, chat groups, or other tools to achieve similar goals?

Activity	Day + Time
1.	
2.	
3.	
4.	

The 30 Day Job Search Survival Guide

Day 18
Most Wanted General Skills

1.	3.	5.
2.	4.	6.

Most Wanted Industry Skills

1.	3.	5.
2.	4.	6.

Tré Rodriguez

Day 18
Skills I Want to Gain or Improve

1.	2.

How I Can Gain These Skills

1.	3.	5.
2.	4.	6.

The 30 Day Job Search Survival Guide

Day 19
Reading List

1.	6.
2.	7.
3.	8.
4.	9.
5.	10.

Tré Rodriguez

Day 20
Potential Interview Questions

1.

2.

3.

4.

5.

6.

7.

8.

The 30 Day Job Search Survival Guide

9.

10.

11.

12.

13.

14.

15.

Tré Rodriguez

Day 21
Video Interview Preparation Checklist

1.	Ensure all hardware is functioning properly.	
2.	Locate and test the necessary software.	
3.	Verify a reliable internet connection.	
4.	Confirm appointment date and time-zone.	
5.	Test and review screen area with a camera.	
6.	Arrange a quiet atmosphere for good audio.	
7.	Negotiate uninterrupted time for privacy.	

The 30 Day Job Search Survival Guide

Day 22
Confront Your Bias

My Identities	Preferences or Prejudices That Are Possible to Hold Related to These Indentities

Tré Rodriguez

Day 23
Interview Follow-Up Questions

1.

2.

3.

4.

5.

The 30 Day Job Search Survival Guide

Day 24
Thank You Note Checklist

	Person to Thank	Company or Association	Email	X
1.				
2.				
3.				
4.				
5.				
6.				
7.				
8.				
9.				
10.				
11.	+			

Tré Rodriguez

Day 25
Salary Research List

	Job Title	Industry	Salary Range
1.			
2.			
3.			
4.			
5.			
6.			
7.			
8.			

The 30 Day Job Search Survival Guide

Day 26
Alternative Compensation

	Non-Monetary Compensation Items That I Would Value
1.	
2.	
3.	
4.	
5.	
6.	
7.	
8.	
9.	
10.	
11.	
12.	
13.	
14.	
15.	

Tré Rodriguez

Counter Offer Feedback Tracking

Cover Letter	Feedback From	Comments Made	X When Feedback Integrated
1.			
2.			
3.			
4.			

The 30 Day Job Search Survival Guide

Day 27
Professional Organizations

1.	
2.	
3.	
4.	

Tré Rodriguez

Day 28
Reasons to Relocate

Pros	Cons

The 30 Day Job Search Survival Guide

Day 28
About Relocation City, State, or Country

Must Have	Nice to Have	Do Not Want

Relocation Terms

Must Have	Nice to Have	Do Not Want

Tré Rodriguez

Day 29
Laid Off or Fired Quick Start Resolution Check List

1.	Get yourself into a supportive or at least neutral atmosphere to process what just happened.
2.	Contact a trusted person from your support network to share the news.
3.	Assess your financial situation and the impact the event will have.
4.	Review any literature or information that was provided during the letting go.
5.	Review the city or state's unemployment website and become familiar with its resources.
6.	If applicable, contact your alma mater(s) career services.
7.	Create or follow a job search plan. For example, the 30 Day Job Search Survival Guide

The 30 Day Job Search Survival Guide

Day 30
General Questions

	Question	Your comments
1.	What has gone well during my job search? Why has it gone well?	
2.	What success have I had? What contributed to that success?	
3.	What has not gone so well during my job search? Why has it not gone so well?	
4.	Have I had any failures? What can I learn from my failures? What can I do to increase the likelihood of my succeeding next time I try?	

Tré Rodriguez

Specific Questions

Ch.	Topic	Question	Your Comments & Adjustments
1.	*Do Nothing*	Are the activities that you chose supporting you in staying calm and happy? If not, what can you change to make them more effective?	
2.	*Set Up a Routine*	Have you been keeping your routine? Does it help? If not, what adjustments can you make to improve it?	
3.	*Build Your Team*	Are the people on your list available and supportive? Have you called on them and received satisfactory responses? If not, do you need to add or subtract people, or change your approach?	

The 30 Day Job Search Survival Guide

4.	Ideal Job Profile	It's time to update your Ideal Job Profile with the new information you've learned or identified through this process. What has changed or become more specific for you?	
5.	Informational Interview	Have you been able to conduct at least one informational interview? If not, why not? What can you do to ensure that you are taking this valuable step to gather information?	
6.	Resume	Have you updated your resume? Did you ask anyone for feedback? Did you make improvements based on their commentary? If not, how can you move forward on this step?	

Tré Rodriguez

7.	*Get Active, Get Outdoors*	Have you been able to spend at least ten minutes per day outdoors? Does your list of activities need to be updated with items that will motivate you more? Could adding a partner to your activities help? How can you ensure this will happen?	
8.	*Cover Letter*	Did you make a least three cover letter drafts and get feedback on them from people you trust? If not, why not? What can you do to be sure that you are getting the CL practice you need?	
9.	*Google Yourself*	Did you Google yourself? Were the results satisfactory? If not, what actions have you taken to improve them?	

The 30 Day Job Search Survival Guide

10.	*LinkedIn Profile*	How does your LinkedIn profile look? Did you spend at least eight hours updating it, making sure that it is complete and polished as possible? If not, why not?	
11.	*Personal Website*	Have you made at least a simple personal website to improve your search results and online presence? If not, what is holding you back? What can you do today to start the process?	
12.	*Ask for Help*	Have you sent an email to all of your contacts asking for support? If yes, what were the results? Have you followed-up on any offered help?	

Tré Rodriguez

13.	*Actual Job Searching*	How is your job searching going? How often are you applying to jobs? Are you reaching at least a 30% return rate on resumes submitted? If not, what can you do to improve your return rate?	
14.	*Give Back*	Have you identified ten people, groups, or organizations that are in need of your help? Have you contributed in some way, however small, to at least one of them? If not, why not?	
15.	*Recruiters & Staffing Agencies*	Have you contacted at least one staffing agency or recruiter? If not, why not?	

The 30 Day Job Search Survival Guide

16.	*Check-In*	Did you complete the check-in from Chapter 16? Did it help you refine your job searching actions? If yes, how? If no, why not?	
17.	*Get Social*	Have you been participating in at least one social activity since you started reading this guide? Why or why not? What can you do to increase your likelihood to do so?	
18.	*Developing Yourself*	Have you undertaken steps to continue your self-development? What did you do and how did it go? If you haven't, what barrier is holding you back and how can you remove it?	

Tré Rodriguez

19.	*Read*	Have you been reading at least ten pages per day? What have you read and what have you gained from the experience? If you haven't, why not?	
20.	*Interview Skills*	Have you worked to improve your interview skills? What impact has this had on your confidence and comfort level? If you haven't, what has stopped you?	
21.	*Video Interview*	Have you worked through the video interview checklist? If not, why not?	

The 30 Day Job Search Survival Guide

22.	*Confront Your Bias*	Have you spent any time considering the conscious and unconscious biases you might hold regarding your job search? How has this helped you to be more objective? If you haven't, why not?	
23.	*Turn the Tables*	Have you thought about the characteristics that you are looking for in your ideal job? Have you drafted a list of questions you can ask an inteviewer?	
25.	*Salary Negotiation*	Have you done your research so that you know the market rate for your profession and industry? Has this increased your confidence when you consider negotiating your value? If you haven't, why not?	

Tré Rodriguez

26.	*Counter Offer*	Have you spent some time considering what non-monetary compensation you would appreciate? If not, why not?	
27.	*Organizations & Certifications*	Have you done any research to find out what professional organizations or certifications would be beneficial to you in your profession and industry? If yes, have you taken steps to join an organization or begin a certification? If not, why not?	
28.	*Relocation*	Have you considered whether or not relocation is an option for you and under what circumstances you would agree to it? If not, why not?	

The 30 Day Job Search Survival Guide

29.	*Fired or Laid Off*	If you have not been fired or laid off, your only goal here is to do the thought experiment of what would happen if you were. Take a few minutes and reflect about the steps you would take.	
30.	*Final Review*	Did you complete the final review? Was it insightful to consider your engagement in the process? How did you benefit from keeping yourself accountable, if at all? If not, why not?	

www.ingramcontent.com/pod-product-compliance
Lightning Source LLC
Chambersburg PA
CBHW052345220526
45465CB00003BA/961